TEC893

Listen, Make, & Learn at STORYTIME

Linking Stories, Crafts, and Literacy Skills

Picture books. They are deceptively simple—often only about 32 pages of limited text—but they are one of the most valuable teaching tools for young children. Storytimes that feature high-quality picture books help build a strong foundation for literacy skills and do so in a fun, kid-pleasing context!

How does storytime promote literacy?

Long before children enter school, books play a powerful role in many of their lives. In fact, children who are read to frequently are more likely to be successful readers than youngsters who have not had many experiences with books.

Storytime affects reading achievement in many ways. It takes young listeners on exciting literary adventures and introduces them to people, places, and things that they might never have contact with otherwise. These reading experiences build students' background knowledge, a key factor in comprehension. Storytime also exposes children to literary structure and style. Exposure to the rhythm, sound, and imagery in literature helps prepare (and inspire!) students to become lifelong readers and writers.

Storytime
- develops reading, writing, listening, and speaking skills
- expands vocabularies
- teaches students about a variety of people, places, and things
- extends students' thinking and stretches their imagination
- models the language and structure of books
- hooks students on reading

What kinds of picture books work well for storytime?

The vast number of children's books means that teachers have access to a tremendous supply of storytime materials! It also means that deciding which of the many books to use with young children might pose a challenge. Consider the following suggestions when making storytime choices.

Look for picture books that have
- well-developed story structures
- rhyming, repetitive, cumulative, or other predictable formats
- plots or themes that students can relate to
- interesting characters
- illustrations that enhance and match the text
- kid-appealing concepts that promote thinking

How can you help students get the most from storytime?

Listening to a good book can be an emotionally rewarding activity, and what a listener takes from the experience can be readily enhanced. Try these quick and easy ideas for enriching storytime.

- **Check and build on prior knowledge.**
  Before reading, prompt discussion or conduct a brief activity that will help students connect information in the book to what they already know.

- **Set a purpose for reading.**
  Ask students to listen for certain details or to check predictions as you read. Establishing such a purpose focuses students' attention and prompts them to be active listeners.

- **Read with expression and enthusiasm.**
  Have fun with storytime! Expressive reading aids comprehension, and it gives students a great example of how fluent readers sound. Plus, a teacher who models a love of literature motivates students to seek out books!

- **Follow up with related activities or discussions.**
  Encourage personal responses to books. Sometimes a very brief discussion is suitable and other times a more developed activity works well. When considering follow-up activities, keep in mind that young children often express and explore ideas best through pictures and other visuals. Ensure that craft-related activities are provided in addition to opportunities for oral and written responses.
  During a follow-up discussion, ask open-ended questions that allow for a variety of responses. Ask students what other books the story reminds them of and why. Or have them compare story events to experiences of their own. When students reflect on questions such as these, their understanding is increased and critical thinking is reinforced.

About This Book

Listen, Make, & Learn at Storytime features 46 high-quality picture books. The reproducible parent notes on page 192 make it easy for you to let parents know the specific books you are sharing with students. They also give parents a great way to prompt discussions with their children about school (and great books!).

Each picture book in this handy resource is presented in a four-page unit that links literature, crafts, and literacy! Each unit has the features described below.

Synopsis

A brief summary highlights the book's distinguishing characteristics. Each book was available at the time of publication. If you have difficulty locating any of the featured titles, check with your library media specialist for assistance.

Skills

Each picture book provides an excellent context for reinforcing a variety of literacy skills. The focus of each unit is noted in an eye-catching graphic. Also, the following skills are reinforced in every unit:
- listening for a purpose
- following directions
- increasing vocabulary by listening, discussing, and/or responding to books

Teacher Preparation and Student Materials

Any needed preparation and materials are listed for easy reference. Minimal teacher preparation is required. All materials are commonly used in schools, are inexpensive to purchase, or are typical throwaway items that can be collected at home. A materials request form is provided on page 7 for your convenience.

Begin With a Book

During the book introduction, the stage is set for the story, and students' prior knowledge is prompted. A purpose for listening guides students to be actively engaged during the read-aloud.

Continue With a Craft

Directions for a follow-up project that students can make with teacher guidance are provided in two step-by-step formats. One format is for teacher reference and one format is designed for student use. The student directions are accompanied by illustrations to help promote the development of independent reading skills. The directions also help students understand that reading can serve a purpose—to make a nifty craft, in this case! The finished project is a tangible reminder of the story. It provides a great starting point for parent-child discussions and helps answer the question "What did you read about in school today?"

Link With a Literacy Skill

The culminating activity strengthens learning by connecting the book, the craft, and essential literacy skills. Because the activity is based on a story, students have a context in which to place their new learning, making it easier for them to retain newly acquired skills.

Reproducible

Any needed patterns are provided. For units that do not require patterns, a related skill sheet offers further reinforcement.

TEC893

From Your Friends at The MAILBOX®

Listen, Make, & Learn at STORYTIME

Linking Stories, Crafts, and Literacy Skills

Writers: Beth Allison, Teresa Aten, Cynthia Barber, Susan Bunyan, Susan DeRiso, Lucia Kemp Henry, Angie Kutzer, Kimberly Love, Gail Marsh, Diane McGraw, Suzanne Moore, Beverly Peerson, Dawn Spurck
Project Manager: Amy Erickson
Staff Editors: Deborah G. Swider, Allison E. Ward
Copy Editors: Sylvan Allen, Gina Farago, Karen Brewer Grossman, Karen L. Huffman, Amy Kirtley-Hill, Debbie Shoffner
Cover Artists: Nick Greenwood, Clevell Harris
Art Coordinators: Pam Crane, Kimberly Richard
Artists: Pam Crane, Theresa Lewis Goode, Nick Greenwood, Clevell Harris, Sheila Krill, Mary Lester, Clint Moore, Greg D. Rieves, Rebecca Saunders, Barry Slate, Stuart Smith, Donna K. Teal
Typesetters: Lynette Dickerson, Mark Rainey

President, The Mailbox Book Company™: Joseph C. Bucci
Director of Book Planning and Development: Chris Poindexter
Book Development Managers: Stephen Levy, Elizabeth H. Lindsay, Thad McLaurin, Susan Walker
Curriculum Director: Karen P. Shelton
Traffic Manager: Lisa K. Pitts
Librarian: Dorothy C. McKinney
Editorial and Freelance Management: Karen A. Brudnak
Editorial Training: Irving P. Crump
Editorial Assistants: Terrie Head, Hope Rodgers, Jan E. Witcher

www.themailbox.com

Table of Contents

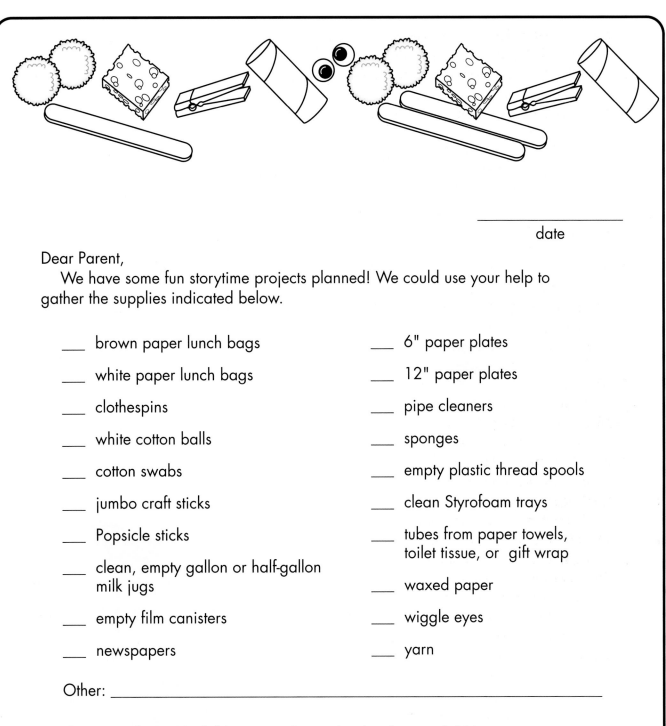

_____
date

Dear Parent,
    We have some fun storytime projects planned! We could use your help to gather the supplies indicated below.

___ brown paper lunch bags

___ white paper lunch bags

___ clothespins

___ white cotton balls

___ cotton swabs

___ jumbo craft sticks

___ Popsicle sticks

___ clean, empty gallon or half-gallon milk jugs

___ empty film canisters

___ newspapers

___ 6" paper plates

___ 12" paper plates

___ pipe cleaners

___ sponges

___ empty plastic thread spools

___ clean Styrofoam trays

___ tubes from paper towels, toilet tissue, or gift wrap

___ waxed paper

___ wiggle eyes

___ yarn

Other: _____

Please send any available materials to school with your child by _____.
I appreciate your help!   date

Sincerely,

_____
teacher signature

Note to the teacher: Make one copy of this page and then program it with the appropriate information. Give each student a copy of the programmed sheet to take home at the beginning of the year or at any time that supplies are needed for a project in this book.

7

The Apple Pie Tree

Written by Zoe Hall
Illustrated by Shari Halpern

Two young sisters delight in observing the seasonal changes of their family's cherished apple tree. From winter to autumn, inviting collage illustrations and simple text depict how the tree transforms and eventually provides the family with the best part of an apple pie. This charming story concludes with an explanation of bee pollination and a tempting four-step recipe.

Skill: Sequence story events.

Teacher Preparation

Literature selection: Preview a copy of *The Apple Pie Tree* and obtain a real apple to help introduce the book. (If desired, gather enough apples to provide a class snack of apple wedges at a chosen point in the unit.)

Craft:
• Set out a shallow container of red tempera paint and several apples cut in half lengthwise.

• Cover students' work area with newspaper for easy cleanup if desired.

• Gather the remaining student materials listed below.

• Make a copy of page 11 for each student to use for the literacy link activity described on page 9.

Student Materials

Each student needs the following:
• copy of page 10
• 6" x 18" strip of construction paper
• 5" square of white construction paper
• 3" square of green construction paper
• access to an apple half
• red tempera paint
• 1" length of brown pipe cleaner
• pencil
• crayon or fine-tipped marker
• scissors
• glue

Step 1

Begin With a Book

The Apple Pie Tree

Whet students' appetites for sequencing with this "a-peeling" story! First, show students an apple and invite them to tell what they know about this fruit, including where it comes from and its uses. Next, display the book cover and read the title. Prompt a class discussion to explore students' ideas about whether a tree can grow an apple pie. As you read the book aloud, ask students to listen carefully to determine why the author might have chosen this title. At the end of the story, lead students to understand that the tree does not produce apple pies, but it does produce their key ingredient—apples. Then give each student the materials listed on page 8. Have him refer to the illustrated directions as you use the steps below to guide him in making a booklet that's ripe for the pickin'!

Step 2

Continue With a Craft

Apple-Print Booklet

Directions:
1. Have each student dip the cut side of an apple into the paint and then press it on the white paper square to make a print. Let the print dry.
2. To make a booklet, have him accordion-fold his paper strip into four panels.
3. Instruct him to cut out the dried print and then glue it on the top panel of the closed booklet.
4. Have him draw a leaf on the green paper, cut it out, and glue it to the apple print. Ask him to glue on the pipe cleaner length to make a stem.
5. Instruct him to title and sign the booklet cover with a crayon or marker.

Step 3

Link With a Literacy Skill

Seasonal Sequencing

Now that your students have a better understanding of how an apple tree changes throughout the year, no doubt they'll be eager to share the information in their apple-print booklets! Use the book's illustrations to review with students the sequence of the seasons and the tree's corresponding changes. Then give each youngster a copy of page 11. Lead the class in chorally reading the sentences. To complete his booklet, each student colors his patterns. He cuts them out, sequences them beginning with the winter scene, and numbers them in the provided boxes. Then he unfolds his booklet, sequentially glues each page on a panel, and refolds the booklet. Encourage each student to take his booklet home for bushels of more reading fun!

My Apple Tree

by Sam

4

This is my apple tree in fall.

Apple-Print Booklet

Follow the directions.

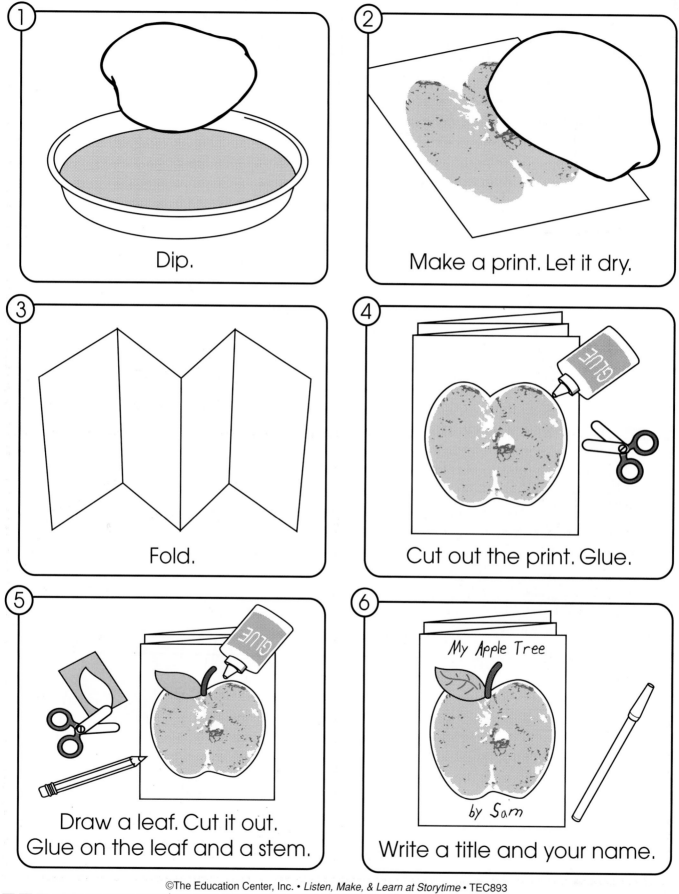

1 Dip.

2 Make a print. Let it dry.

3 Fold.

4 Cut out the print. Glue.

5 Draw a leaf. Cut it out. Glue on the leaf and a stem.

6 My Apple Tree by Sam Write a title and your name.

Note to the teacher: Use with *The Apple Pie Tree* unit that begins on page 8.

This is my apple tree in winter.

This is my apple tree in summer.

This is my apple tree in spring.

This is my apple tree in fall.

Aunt Flossie's Hats (and Crab Cakes Later)

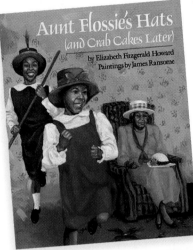

Written by Elizabeth Fitzgerald Howard
Illustrated by James Ransome

Sarah and her sister love their visits with Great-great-aunt Flossie because they always include a delicious treat and a peek into her intriguing hatboxes. Each hat holds a special memory for Aunt Flossie, who enjoys telling about the memory as much as the girls enjoy listening to its story. Young listeners will delight in the stories within the story as well as the vibrant oil-painted illustrations that depict Baltimore's African American heritage.

Skill: Illustrate and tell about an event in the correct sequence.

Teacher Preparation

Literature selection: Preview a copy of *Aunt Flossie's Hats (and Crab Cakes Later)*. Obtain a decorative lidded box, such as a hatbox, that is large enough to hold the book. Place the book inside it.

Craft:

• Set out a variety of decorative stickers.

• Gather the remaining student materials listed below.

• For each student, cut a 2½" x 11" strip of white paper to use with the literacy link on the following page.

Student Materials

Each student needs the following:
• copy of pages 14 and 15
• 6" x 9" piece of construction paper
• access to a variety of decorative stickers
• pencil
• crayons
• scissors
• glue
• access to a stapler

Begin With a Book

Aunt Flossie's Hats (and Crab Cakes Later)

Aunt Flossie has boxes and boxes of hats and each one reminds her of a different occasion! Confirm that students understand what a memory is. Then display the prepared box and tell them that some people use boxes such as this one to hold memories. Invite youngsters to share their ideas about how a box might serve this purpose. Then, with a great deal of fanfare, open the box and remove the book. Explain that a character in the book has many memories tucked away in boxes. During an oral reading of the book, ask students to listen carefully to learn about the character's special memories. To help each student create her own box full of memories, distribute the materials listed on page 12. Have her refer to the illustrated steps as you use the directions below to help her complete her project.

Step 1

Continue With a Craft

Beautiful Box

Directions:
1. Have each student write her name on the lid. Then ask her to color the box and lid.
2. Instruct her to cut out the box, lid, and pocket.
3. Direct her to position the pocket on the box and staple it in place.
4. Have her fold back the top edge of the lid. Help her glue the box to it so that the lid can be lifted to "open" the box.
5. Have her glue the closed box to the construction paper.
6. Invite her to decorate the box and lid with stickers.

Step 2

Link With a Literacy Skill

Sharing Special Memories

Stories such as Aunt Flossie's provide plenty of inspiration to fill each child's memory box! Encourage each student to recall a day that was special for her. To capture the memory, give her a precut paper strip. Instruct her to accordion-fold the strip into four panels. Have her illustrate each panel to tell about the main events of the special day in sequential order. Instruct the child to refold the resulting mini booklet and tuck it into the pocket on her box.

During a group time, invite each child, in turn, to open her memory box and remove her booklet. Have her "read" the pictures aloud, inserting additional details in the appropriate sequence to enhance her classmates' understanding of the memory. Encourage each child to take her memorable project home to share with her family.

Step 3

Beautiful Box

Follow the directions.

1. Write. Color.

2. Cut.

3. Staple.

4. Fold on the line. Glue.

5. Glue.

6. Decorate.

©The Education Center, Inc. • *Listen, Make, & Learn at Storytime* • TEC893

Note to the teacher: Use with the *Aunt Flossie's Hats (and Crab Cakes Later)* unit that begins on page 12.

Patterns
Use with the *Aunt Flossie's Hats
(and Crab Cakes Later)* unit
that begins on page 12.

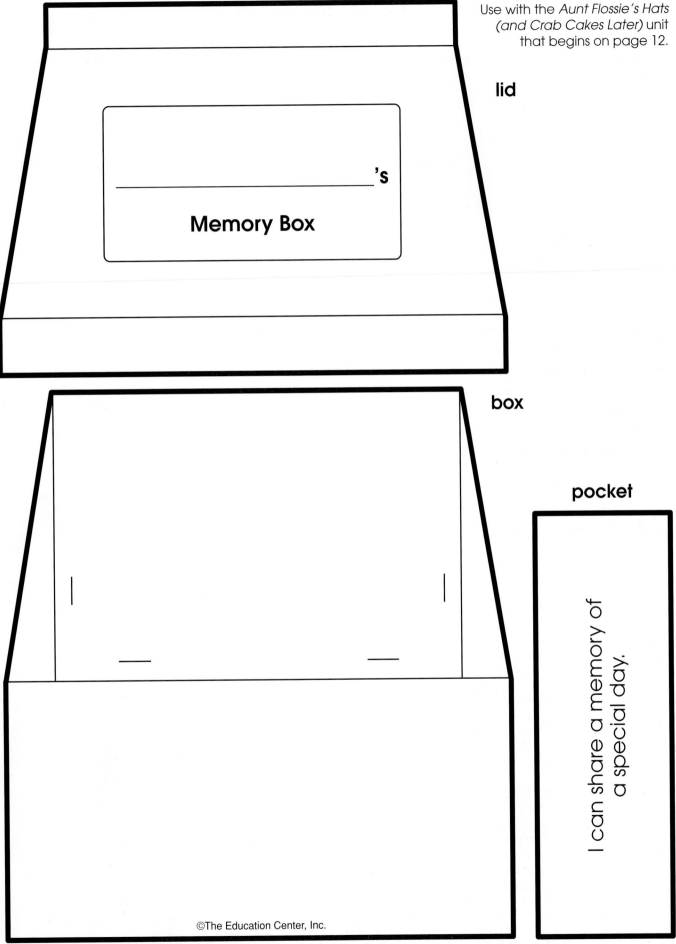

lid

_____'s

Memory Box

box

pocket

I can share a memory of a special day.

©The Education Center, Inc.

Barn Dance!

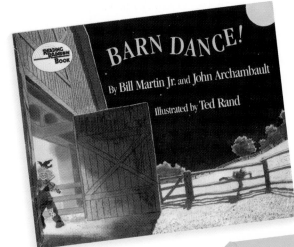

Written by Bill Martin Jr. and John Archambault
Illustrated by Ted Rand

What's that sound coming from the cornfield? Why it's a toe-tappin' hoedown! The rhythmic plink, plink, plink of a scarecrow's fiddle lures a boy from his bed to a spirited barn dance. The boy and a flock of sprightly farm critters delight in a-rockin' and a-sockin' until morning nears and the magic time ends.

Skills: Listen for rhythm and rhyme. Produce rhyming words.

Teacher Preparation

Literature selection: Preview a copy of *Barn Dance!* to practice reading the rhythmic text. Obtain a recording of "Turkey in the Straw" or a selected bluegrass song.

Craft:

• For each student, slightly overlap two six-inch paper plates and staple them into place.

• Set out brown tempera paint and paintbrushes.

• Cover students' work area with newspaper for easy cleanup.

• Gather the remaining student materials listed on this page.

• Collect a class supply of unsharpened pencils for the literacy link on the following page.

Extension: If desired, make a copy of page 19 for each student to complete at the conclusion of the literacy link activity described on page 17.

Student Materials

Each student needs the following:
• copy of page 18
• prepared paper plates (See instructions above.)
• 1½" x 15" strip of brown construction paper
• 2" square of black construction paper
• 1½" x 3" piece of black construction paper
• access to brown tempera paint and a paintbrush
• permanent marker
• glue
• scissors

16

Begin With a Book

Barn Dance!

Step 1

Yee-haw! It's time for some rousing reading fun! Play a recording of "Turkey in the Straw" (or a suitable substitute), inviting students to clap their hands to the beat. Explain that the words in the featured book have a catchy beat much like the song does. As you read the book aloud, ask students to listen to how the rhyming text gives the story rhythm. Then revisit the page that shows a close-up view of the scarecrow. Verify that students know the name of the instrument he is playing. Explain that they will each make a pretend fiddle for a rhyming activity. Provide each youngster with the materials listed on page 16. Ask him to refer to the illustrated steps as you help him complete his project.

Continue With a Craft

A Fine Fiddle

Step 2

Directions:
1. Instruct the child to paint the backs of the prepared paper plates brown. Allow the paint to dry.
2. To make fiddle strings, ask the student to draw lines along the paper strip with a marker.
3. Direct him to glue the strip along the center of the plates so that it extends approximately six inches beyond them.
4. Have him cut the paper square in half diagonally to make two triangles. Instruct him to glue one triangle on the fiddle so that it covers the end of the strip. Ask him to discard the other triangle.
5. Instruct him to cut the paper rectangle in half lengthwise. Direct him to turn his project over and glue the two strips to the fiddle to resemble tuning pegs.

Link With a Literacy Skill

Time to Rhyme!

Step 3

After "visiting" the hoedown in *Barn Dance!*, no doubt your students will want to create some foot-stompin' rhymes of their own! Write on the chalkboard a familiar word that rhymes with several other words. As students brainstorm rhyming words, list them on the board. Next, ask students to stand with their fiddles. Clap your hands to establish a beat and encourage students to tap their toes in time to it. Keeping the beat, recite the lines shown. Then lead students in a choral reading of the list as each youngster uses an unsharpened pencil to "play" his fiddle. Repeat the process with a desired number of other student-generated rhyming lists. A toe-tappin' time will be had by all!

Cheery Chant

Play your fiddle right on time.

Tap your toes and name a rhyme!

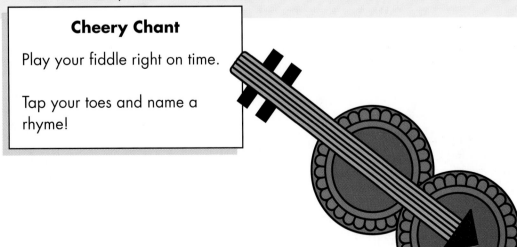

A Fine Fiddle

Follow the directions.

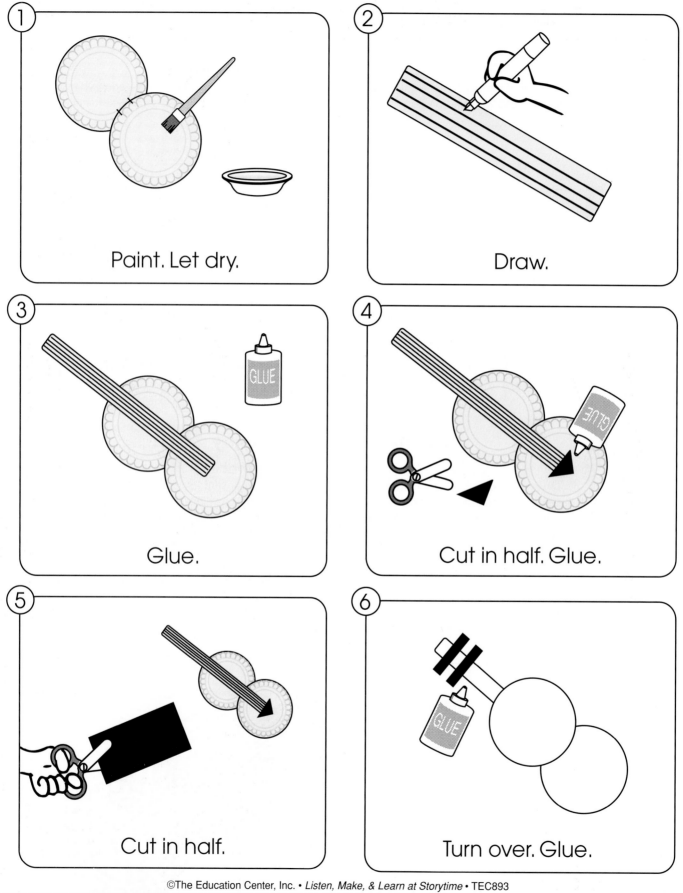

1. Paint. Let dry.

2. Draw.

3. Glue.

4. Cut in half. Glue.

5. Cut in half.

6. Turn over. Glue.

©The Education Center, Inc. • *Listen, Make, & Learn at Storytime* • TEC893

Note to the teacher: Use with the *Barn Dance!* unit that begins on page 16.

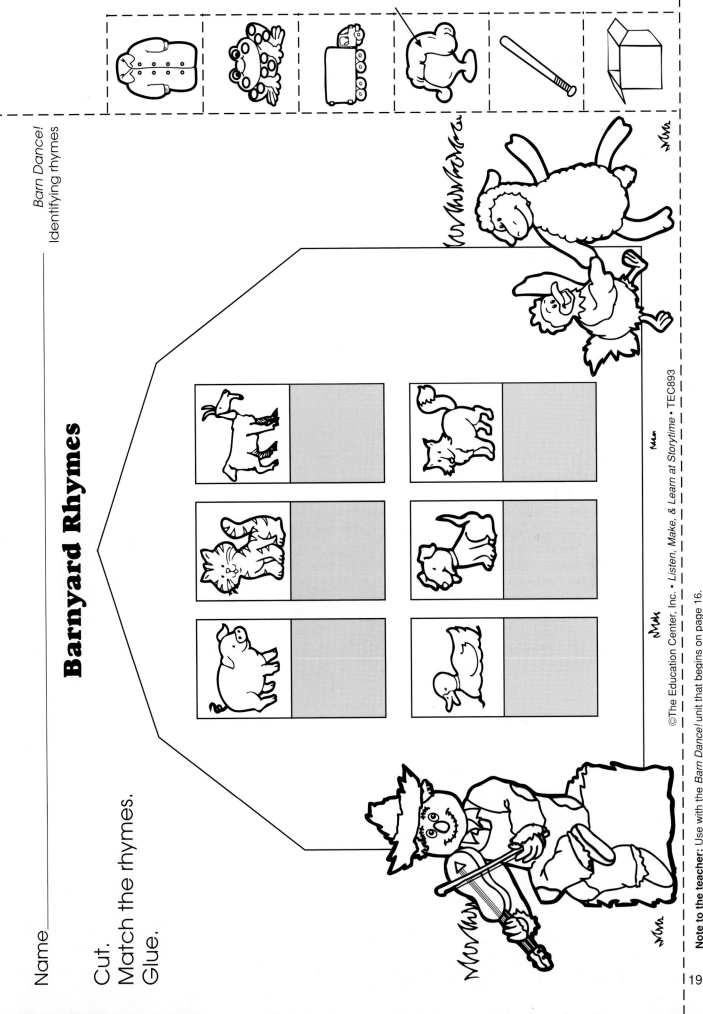

Barnyard Rhymes

Name

Cut.
Match the rhymes.
Glue.

Note to the teacher: Use with the *Barn Dance!* unit that begins on page 16.

19

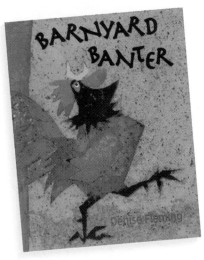

Barnyard Banter

Written and illustrated by Denise Fleming

The noisy barnyard animals are all in their expected places. All except Goose, that is! An irresistible combination of onomatopoeia and rhyming text leads the farm critters in a playful romp across the bold handmade-paper illustrations as readers search for Goose.

Skill: Join in a choral reading.

Teacher Preparation

Literature selection: Preview a copy of *Barnyard Banter*.

Craft:

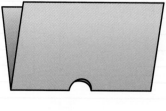

- For each student, fold a 9" x 12" sheet of construction paper in half. Cut a small half circle in the center of the fold as shown.

- Gather the remaining student materials listed below.

Student Materials

Each student needs the following:
- copy of pages 22 and 23
- prepared 9" x 12" sheet of construction paper (See instructions above.)
- flexible drinking straw
- crayons
- scissors
- glue
- tape

Begin With a Book

Barnyard Banter

The pigs, cows, and kittens are all accounted for, but has anyone seen Goose? To prepare youngsters to join in a rollicking search for Goose, display the book cover and read the title aloud. Write a student-generated list of barnyard animals on the chalkboard. Next, explain that *banter* means "to talk in a playful way." Point out that farm animals do not talk, but they make sounds to communicate. Invite students to identify the sound made by each of the listed animals. Ask students to listen carefully as you read the book aloud to find out what animals and sounds the author has included in the story. To prepare for a choral reading of the story, give each student the materials listed on page 20. Have her refer to the illustrated directions as you use the steps below to guide her in making a handy story prop.

Step 1

Continue With a Craft

Where's Goose?

Step 2

Directions:
1. Have each student color the patterns.
2. Ask her to cut out the grid and the goose card.
3. Direct her to glue the short sides of the prepared construction paper to make a pocket.
4. Instruct her to position the pocket so that the cut opening is on the bottom. Then have her glue the grid on it.
5. Tell her to stretch out the straw. Have her turn the goose card facedown and tape one end of the straw near the bottom of the card.
6. Have her vertically position the straw in the pocket and pull the untaped end through the cut opening.

Link With a Literacy Skill

Honk, Honk, Honk!

Step 3

Students' completed projects provide a picture-perfect way to follow along during a choral reading of this barnyard tale. Ask each youngster to use one hand to hold her project by the base, keeping her other hand free. As you slowly reread the story, direct her to point to the appropriate animals on her project and join in the reading. When Goose is found at the end of the story, ask her to use her free hand to push up the straw to reveal her goose card. Then invite her to exclaim, "There's Goose! Honk, honk, honk!" Encourage her to take her project home and use it to retell the story to her family. Now that's a barnyard full of literacy fun!

Where's Goose?

Follow the directions.

① Color.

② Cut.

③ Glue.

④ Glue.

⑤ Tape.

⑥ Pull the straw through the hole.

Note to the teacher: Use with the *Barnyard Banter* unit that begins on page 20.

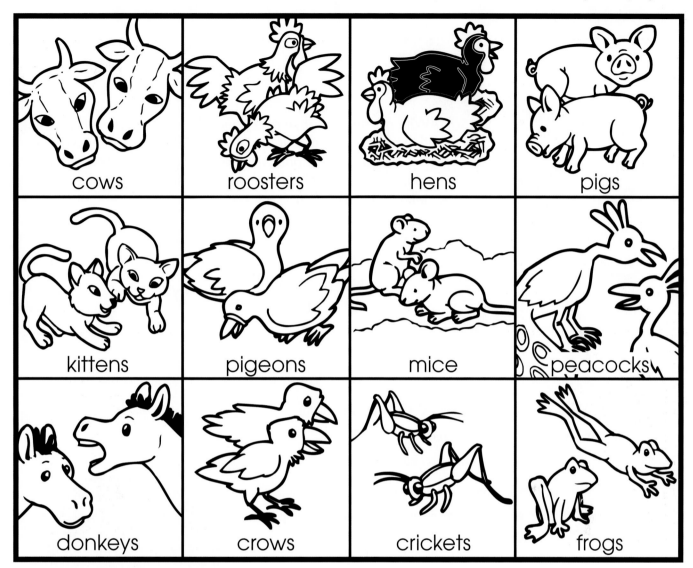

cows

roosters

hens

pigs

kittens

pigeons

mice

peacocks

donkeys

crows

crickets

frogs

Goose

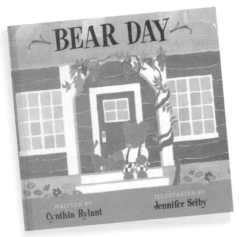

Bear Day

Written by Cynthia Rylant
Illustrated by Jennifer Selby

With rhythm and rhyme, a young bear completes his morning routine and then goes out for the day. After a pleasant walk and picnic, he goes home and prepares to do it all again the next day. The soft illustrations and predictable circular story make this an excellent read-aloud choice for young children.

Skills: Sequence story events. Dramatize a story.

Teacher Preparation

Literature selection: Preview a copy of *Bear Day.*

Craft:

- Set out a container of orange tempera paint.

- Cover students' work area with newspaper for easy cleanup, if desired.

- Gather the remaining student materials listed below.

- For the literacy link on the next page, collect the following storytelling props: a blanket and pillow, a washcloth and towel, a backpack and stuffed bear, several plastic fruits, and a scarf.

Extension: If desired, make a copy of page 27 for each student to complete at the conclusion of the literacy link activity described on page 25.

Student Materials

Each student needs the following:
- copy of page 26
- 6" paper plate
- two 2¹/₂" orange construction paper circles
- 1" purple construction paper circle
- 3" x 18" strip of orange construction paper
- 2 wiggle eyes
- paintbrush
- access to a stapler
- glue
- orange tempera paint

Begin With a Book

Bear Day

What do you get when you combine an adorable bear and irresistible rhyming text? An endearing story that's perfect for introducing youngsters to story sequence! Before reading, invite each of several volunteers to share three things he did in sequence to get ready for school, such as stretch, wash his face, and get dressed. Tell students that they will hear a story about a bear that also does several things to get ready for the day. Read the book aloud. Then use the book's illustrations to help students sequentially recall the bear's daily activities. For additional reinforcement of story events, distribute the materials listed on page 24. Help each child follow the illustrated directions as you guide him in making a bear headband to use in a retelling of the story.

Continue With a Craft

Bear Headband

Directions:
1. Direct each child to paint the back of his paper plate orange. Allow the paint to dry.
2. Have him glue the ears, nose, and eyes in place.
3. Size the strip to fit the youngster's head and then staple the ends of the strip to the plate.

Link With a Literacy Skill

A "Beary" Good Performance

Here's a "paws-itively" fun way to re-create the bear's activities in sequence! Invite each child to don his headband and join you in a circle. Explain that each child will have a turn pretending to be the bear during one part of the bear's day. Display the storytelling props listed on page 24. For each one, have students recall when a similar item appeared in the book. As you slowly read aloud the first sentence of the story, have a volunteer act it out, using the props as appropriate. Continue in this manner with the remaining sentences until each child has taken a turn. (Repeat the story as needed to allow ample acting time.) Tomorrow is another bear day, so place the book and props in a dramatic-play area for additional sequencing fun!

Bear Headband

Follow the directions.

1. Paint. Let dry.

2. Glue on a nose.

3. Glue on two ears.

4. Glue on two eyes.

5. Ask your teacher to staple.

6. Wear your bear headband!

Note to the teacher: Use with the *Bear Day* unit that begins on page 24.

Name _____

What a Day!

Color.
Cut.
Glue the pictures in order.

Bear Day
Sequencing story events

He waves hello.

The bear wakes up.

He washes his face.

He eats breakfast.

©The Education Center, Inc. • *Listen, Make, & Learn at Storytime* • TEC893

Note to the teacher: Use with the *Bear Day* unit that begins on page 24.

27

The Big Wide-Mouthed Frog

Written and illustrated by Ana Martín Larrañaga

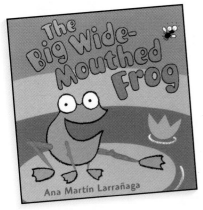

A big wide-mouthed frog sets out to see the world in this humorous tale illustrated with collage and watercolor media. The overconfident amphibian questions several animals about their diets. The frog's cockiness grows with each encounter until he meets a hungry crocodile whose diet includes wide-mouthed frogs. The surprise ending will undoubtedly leave listeners wanting to hear the story again and again!

Skill: Recognize and use complete sentences.

Teacher Preparation

Literature selection: Preview a copy of *The Big Wide-Mouthed Frog.*

Craft:
- Arrange for each child to have a clean, clear plastic milk jug with a lid (gallon or half-gallon size).

- For each student, cut a 1½-inch Styrofoam ball in half.

- Obtain a craft knife for teacher use.

- Gather the remaining student materials listed below.

- Make a copy of page 31 for each student to use for the literacy link on page 29.

Student Materials

Each student needs the following:
- copy of page 30
- clean, clear gallon or half-gallon milk jug
- green tempera paint
- disposable bowl
- 1½" Styrofoam ball cut in half
- small piece of black felt
- permanent black marker
- scissors
- glue

Step 1

Begin With a Book
The Big Wide-Mouthed Frog
Hop right into the story's topic with a class discussion about what frogs eat. As students share their ideas about the diet of most frogs, lead them to conclude that many frogs eat insects, such as flies. Then display the book cover and direct students' attention to the pictured fly. Ask them to look for the fly throughout the book as you read the story aloud. Then, to help each child make a big wide-mouthed frog of her own, distribute the materials listed on page 28. Have each student refer to the illustrated directions as you use the steps below to guide her in completing the project.

Step 2

Continue With a Craft
Froggie Fly Catcher
Directions:
1. Have each student pour a generous amount of green paint into her jug.
2. Ask her to secure the lid on the jug and then shake the jug to completely coat the inside with paint.
3. Direct her to open the jug and invert it over a disposable bowl to allow the excess paint to drain.
4. Instruct her to cut out two small circles from the felt. Have her glue each one on a separate half of a Styrofoam ball and then glue the two halves on the jug to resemble eyes.
5. Ask her to use the marker to draw two nostrils and a big mouth on the jug.
6. Carefully use a craft knife to cut out the mouth of each child's jug. Let the jugs dry overnight in a cool, dry place.

Step 3

Link With a Literacy Skill
Fly Buffet
Have students use their froggie fly catchers to feast on complete sentence identification! Give each student a copy of page 31 and ask her to cut out the patterns. Have her silently read the words on each one. If the words form a complete sentence, direct her to "feed" the fly to her frog. If they do not, have her place the fly beside her frog. After each youngster sorts her flies in this manner and you check her work, pair students. Instruct the students in each twosome to work together to orally complete the incomplete sentences. Invite volunteers to tell the class their favorite sentences. Then have each student place all of her flies in her frog for easy transport. Encourage her to repeat the fly-sorting activity with a family member.

The frog is

green frog is

I see the

Froggie Fly Catcher

Follow the directions.

1. Pour.

2. Put on the lid. Shake.

3. Turn the jug upside down.

4. Cut out the two circles. Glue.

5. Glue.

6. Draw a nose and mouth. Ask the teacher to cut out the mouth.

Note to the teacher: Use with *The Big Wide-Mouthed Frog* unit that begins on page 28.

Patterns

Use with *The Big Wide-Mouthed Frog* unit that begins on page 28.

I see a frog.

I see the

green frog is

The frog is green.

can a frog

Many frogs eat flies.

frog eats a

A frog can hop.

This frog can talk.

The funny frog

Brown Bear, Brown Bear, What Do You See?

Written by Bill Martin Jr.
Illustrated by Eric Carle

A series of colorful (and unusual!) sightings begins when Brown Bear spies a bird in this rhythmic read-aloud. From the red bird to the children, each sight is portrayed with a bold tissue paper collage. Count on young listeners to eagerly anticipate what each animal sees and to chime right in with the predictable text!

Skill: Use color words to describe.

Teacher Preparation

Literature selection: Preview a copy of *Brown Bear, Brown Bear, What Do You See?*

Craft:
- Set out several colors of tempera paint. Provide at least one unlidded, empty film canister for each color of paint.

- Cover students' work area with newspaper for easy cleanup, if desired.

- For each student, cut a triangle from a paper plate. Then staple it to the plate to make a fish as shown.

- Gather the remaining student materials listed below.

Extension: If desired, make a copy of page 35 for each student to complete at the conclusion of the literacy link activity described on page 33.

Student Materials

Each student needs the following:
- copy of page 34
- prepared paper plate (See instructions above.)
- tempera paint
- access to one empty film canister for each color of paint
- paintbrush
- button
- glue

Begin With a Book

Brown Bear, Brown Bear, What Do You See?

Lead your youngsters on an imaginative exploration of color words! Show students the book cover and read the title aloud. Ask them to predict what Brown Bear might see in the story and encourage them to describe the predicted sights by color. Read the book aloud; then have students verbally compare Brown Bear's actual sightings with their predictions.

Next, reread the book, pausing at the color words and encouraging youngsters to chime in. Point out that the author uses only one color word to describe each animal. Remind students that some animals, such as black-and-white cats, are two or more colors. Then distribute the materials listed on page 32. Ask each youngster to refer to the illustrated steps as you use the directions below to help him create his own colorful creature.

Continue With a Craft

Fanciful Fish

Directions:
1. Instruct each student to paint the front of the paper plate one color. Allow the paint to dry.
2. Have him dip the top edge of a film canister in paint. Then ask him to use it to make prints on the plate, applying more paint to the canister as necessary.
3. Invite the youngster to make additional prints with a different color of paint, if desired.
4. Direct him to glue a button on for an eye.

Link With a Literacy Skill

What a Sight!

Everyone knows what Brown Bear sees, but how about what your students see? Find out with this speaking activity, and spin quite a fish story in the process! After each student has made a fish as described above, have students form a large circle. Instruct each youngster to hold his fish so that the front of it is visible to his classmates. Ask a selected student the following question: "[Student's name, student's name], what do you see?" The youngster turns to the student on his left, looks at his classmate's fish, and responds, "I see a [the appropriate colors] fish looking at me." Then he asks the classmate what he sees, using your question as a model.

The question-and-answer pattern continues around the circle until it returns to the first student. To conclude the activity, he says, "I see a whole school of fish looking at me!" Congratulate your young observers on a job well done. Then display their fishy creations on a bulletin board titled "What Do You See Under the Sea?"

Fanciful Fish

Follow the directions.

1 Paint. Let the paint dry.

2 Dip.

3 Make prints.

4 Dip again.

5 Make more prints.

6 Glue.

Note to the teacher: Use with the *Brown Bear, Brown Bear, What Do You See?* unit that begins on page 32.

Name_____

Colors I See

Read.

Color.

red	yellow	green

Read.

Write each color word.

Color.

1. I see a _____ bird.

2. I see a _____ frog.

3. I see a _____ sun.

Bonus Box: Use a blue crayon to make a picture on the back of this sheet. Write a sentence about the picture.

©The Education Center, Inc. • *Listen, Make, & Learn at Storytime* • TEC893

Note to the teacher: Use with the *Brown Bear, Brown Bear, What Do You See?* unit that begins on page 32.

35

Bunny Cakes

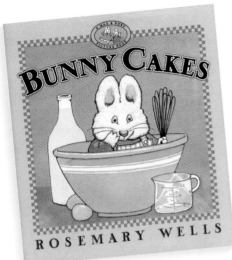

Written and illustrated by Rosemary Wells

Max inadvertently causes some kitchen mishaps as his older sister, Ruby, makes a birthday cake for Grandma. Each time an ingredient needs to be replenished, Ruby jots it down on a grocery list and Max uses his developing writing skills to add a request of his own—Red-Hot Marshmallow Squirters. Youngsters will enjoy seeing Max's communication efforts evolve until he finally makes himself understood with a picture of the much-awaited candy.

Skill: Read words in the -ake word family.

Teacher Preparation

Literature selection: Preview a copy of *Bunny Cakes.*

Craft:

• Make a white construction paper copy of page 39 for each student. Use a craft knife to slit each cake along the dotted lines.

• Pour white glue into a desired number of paint cups.

• Cover students' work area with newspaper for easy cleanup.

• Gather the remaining student materials listed below.

Student Materials

Each student needs the following:
• copy of page 38
• prepared white construction paper copy of page 39 (See instructions above.)
• access to glue and a paintbrush
• variety of cake-decorating sprinkles
• scissors
• crayons
• tape

Begin With a Book

Bunny Cakes

Hmmm—earthworm cake with caterpillar icing or angel surprise cake with raspberry-fluff icing. Which will Grandma prefer? Before reading the book to find out, poll your students to determine their favorite types of cake. Then display the endpapers of the featured book. Use the illustrations to prompt a class discussion about the ingredients, supplies, and steps that are typically needed to make cakes. Tell students that each character in the book makes a special cake. As you read the book aloud, ask students to listen to the words and study the pictures to find out about the cakes. Then distribute the materials listed on page 36. Have each child refer to the illustrated directions as you use the steps below to help her create a unique cake of her own.

Step 1

Continue With a Craft

Create a Cake

Step 2

Directions:
1. Have each student color her cake and plate.
2. Direct her to cut out the cake and strip along the bold lines.
3. Instruct her to paint glue over the frosting. Then have her sprinkle small cake decorations on the wet glue. Help her gently shake off any excess decorations.
4. After the glue is dry, help the student thread the strip through the slits as shown below. Overlap the ends and tape them in place as indicated.

Link With a Literacy Skill

Bake Me a Cake

Step 3

Pat-a-cake, pat-a-cake…forget marking it with a *B*. Your students' cakes are marked with onsets and a rime! Ask students to share their ideas about why Max had difficulty making his request understood but Ruby did not. Lead them to realize that the grocer had an easier time reading Ruby's writing because she used letters to make words. Point out that it takes practice to make words like Ruby did. To provide word-making practice for your students, have each youngster turn the loop on her cake project to make the word *cake*. (If students need assistance, verbally divide the word into its onset and rime; then blend the onset and rime together.) Repeat the process with each of the remaining word possibilities in random order. Then pair students and have them practice making words and reading them to their partners. For more *-ake* word fun, place *Bunny Cakes* in your classroom library. Invite students to find the word *cake* each time it appears in the book. What a tempting way to serve up reading reinforcement!

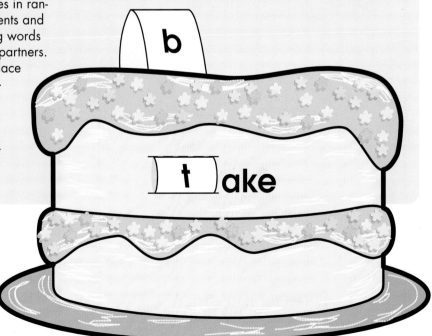

Create a Cake

Follow the directions.

1. Color the cake and plate.

2. Cut out the cake and strip.

3. Paint glue on the frosting.

4. Sprinkle. Let dry.

5. Thread the strip.

6. Tape.

©The Education Center, Inc. • *Listen, Make, & Learn at Storytime* • TEC893

Note to the teacher: Use with the *Bunny Cakes* unit that begins on page 36.

Tape.

b

c

m

t

sh

w

r

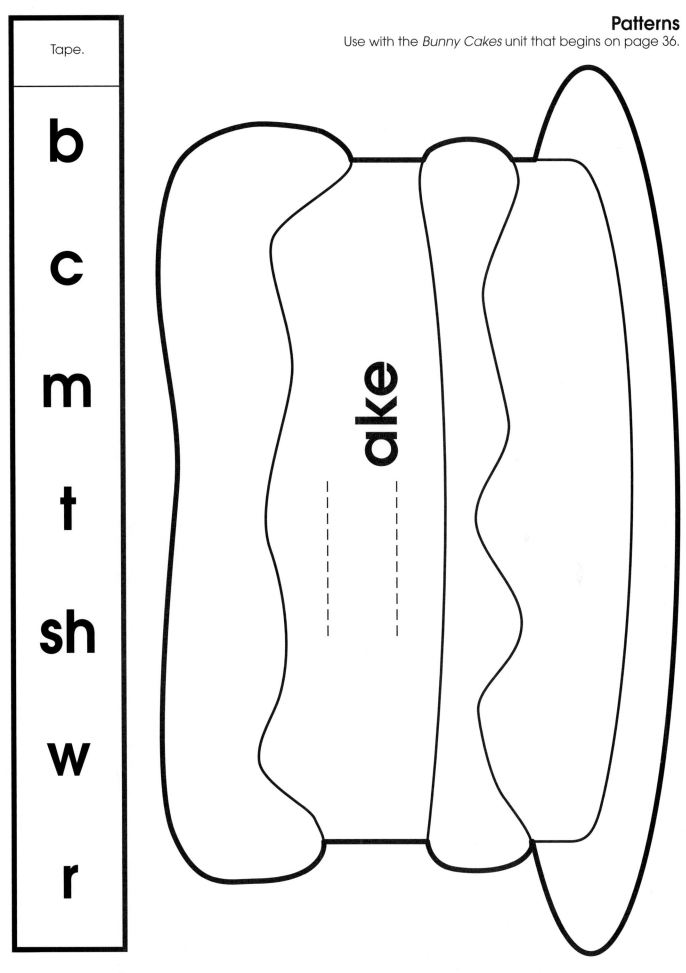

ake

Caps for Sale:
A Tale of a Peddler, Some Monkeys and Their Monkey Business

Told and illustrated by Esphyr Slobodkina

"Caps! Caps for sale! Fifty cents a cap!" A tired cap peddler walks through the town and toward the country with a stack of caps upon his head. In need of rest, he naps beneath a tree full of mischievous monkeys, never suspecting that he'll awaken to a surprising turn of events. Earth-toned illustrations and predictable text help make this classic a favorite among young children.

Skill: Identify the beginning, middle, and end of a story.

Teacher Preparation

Literature selection: Preview a copy of *Caps for Sale.*

Craft:

• Gather the student materials listed below.

Student Materials

Each student needs the following:
• copy of page 42
• 3 different-colored construction paper copies of page 43
• three 6" x 9" sheets of white paper
• button
• crayons
• scissors
• glue
• access to a stapler

Begin With a Book

Caps for Sale

What do you get when you team up a peddler, a stack of caps, and a number of monkeys? A comical sequence of events! Show students the book cover and read the full title aloud. Explain that a *peddler* is a person who sells merchandise door-to-door or on a street. Tell students that the cap peddler in this story carries his merchandise in an unusual way, and ask them to predict his carrying method. Also invite students to share their ideas about the role that monkeys play in the story. Ask students to check their predictions as you share the book. Lead a class discussion to compare the predictions with the story. Then orally summarize the beginning, middle, and end of the story with students' help. For additional practice with story events, give each child the materials listed on page 40. Have him refer to the illustrated directions as you guide him in stacking up the events.

Continue With a Craft

A Stack of Caps

Directions:
1. Have each student cut out his caps.
2. Ask him to staple the top of each cap to a separate sheet of white paper.
3. Instruct him to carefully trim the white paper to the shape of the caps.
4. Direct him to use crayons to embellish each cap as desired.
5. Help him overlap and glue the three caps, being careful to ensure that the top layer of each cap can be lifted. (See the illustration below.)
6. Ask him to glue a button on the top cap.

Link With a Literacy Skill

Under Their Caps

Caps off to story events! As you reread the book, ask students to pay particular attention to what happens at the beginning, middle, and end of the story. Then have each youngster vertically position his cap project on a work surface. Have him lift the cover of the top cap and carefully fold it back to reveal the white paper (provide assistance as necessary). On the white paper, instruct him to write (or illustrate and label) what happens at the beginning of the story. Have him repeat the process with the second and third caps for the middle and end of the story. Provide time for each youngster to share his work with a partner before taking it home. He won't want to keep this picture book follow-up under his cap!

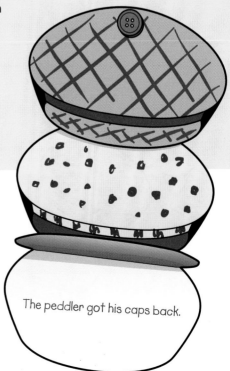

The peddler got his caps back.

41

A Stack of Caps

Follow the directions.

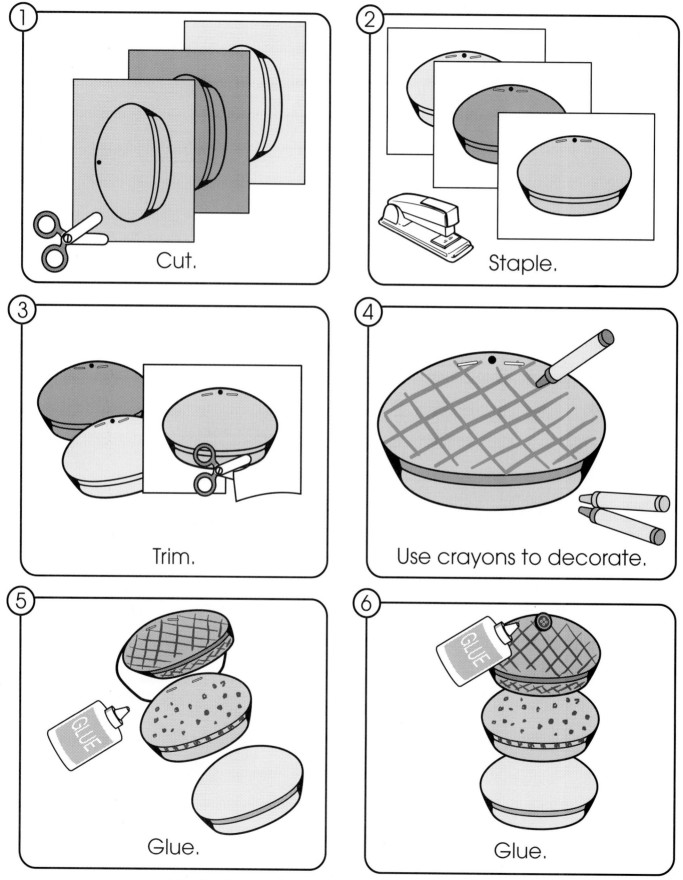

1. Cut.

2. Staple.

3. Trim.

4. Use crayons to decorate.

5. Glue.

6. Glue.

Note to the teacher: Use with the *Caps for Sale* unit that begins on page 40.

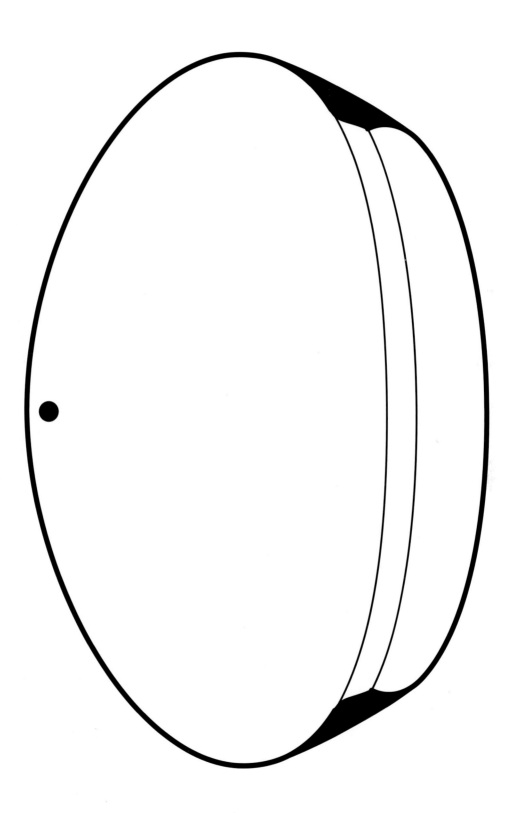

Corduroy

Written and illustrated by Don Freeman

Poor Corduroy! He has been waiting a long time for someone to buy him! When the sad little teddy bear learns that his missing button might hurt his chances of being purchased, he sets off in search of it. But he soon discovers that a young girl named Lisa likes him just the way he is—missing button and all!

Skills: Explore setting, characters, and plot. Retell a story.

Teacher Preparation

Literature selection: Preview a copy of *Corduroy*.

Craft:
- Obtain several empty cardboard tubes, such as those used for toilet tissue or paper towels. Cut the tubes to provide a piece that is approximately 2½ inches long for each student.

- Gather the remaining student materials listed below.

Student Materials

Each student needs the following:
- copy of page 46
- white construction paper copy of page 47
- approximately 2½"-long piece of an empty cardboard tube
- 2" x 4" strip of poster board
- 1" x 4" strip of poster board
- letter-size manila folder
- small button
- gallon-size resealable plastic bag
- crayons
- pencil
- scissors
- glue

Begin With a Book

Corduroy

Launch an investigation of story elements with this "paw-sitively" endearing classic! Show students the book cover and read the title aloud. Invite them to share their ideas about where the pictured bear is. Explain that where and when a story occurs is called the setting. Invite students to predict what will happen in the story. Ask them to listen carefully to check their ideas as you read the story aloud.

At the book's conclusion, have students recall the setting, main characters, and plot. Then, for a kid-pleasing retelling activity, give each youngster the materials listed on page 44. Have her refer to the illustrated steps as you use the directions below to help her make story props.

Step 1

Continue With a Craft

Corduroy and Friends

Directions:
1. Have each student color the character patterns and then cut them out.
2. Instruct her to glue the watchman pattern along the length of the tube and then stand the prop.
3. Direct her to glue the Lisa pattern to the wide poster board strip as shown below. Have her fold back each end of the strip to stand the character. Ask her to use the second strip to prepare the Corduroy prop in the same manner.
4. Have her store the three props and the provided button in the plastic bag. (If desired, continue with the remainder of the project and the literacy link below on another day.)
5. Instruct the youngster to open the folder and place it horizontally on a work surface. Have her use the entire space to illustrate the toy department.
6. Ask her to flip the folder over, illustrate the furniture department, and then close the folder.

Step 2

Link With a Literacy Skill

Act It Out!

Raise the curtain on retelling skills! Use the book's illustrations to review the story's setting, main characters, and plot with students. Next, pair students. Have one child in each twosome open her illustrated folder and stand it. Ask her to use her prepared characters, backdrops, and button to retell the story to her partner. Then direct the partners to trade roles. After every youngster has acted out the story, have her place her characters and button in her bag. Encourage her to take the materials home and use them to tell the story to her family. Now that's a story follow-up sure to get rave reviews!

Step 3

Corduroy and Friends

Follow the directions.

1. Color.

2. Cut out.

3. Glue the watchman. Stand.

4. Glue Lisa onto the big strip. Fold. Stand.

5. Glue Corduroy. Fold. Stand.

6. Put the characters and a button in the bag.

7. Open. Draw and color the toy department.

8. Flip. Draw and color the furniture department.

Note to the teacher: Use with the *Corduroy* unit that begins on page 44.

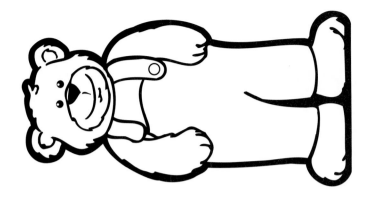

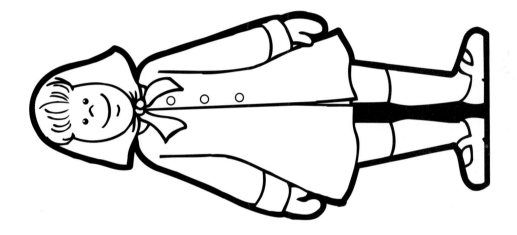

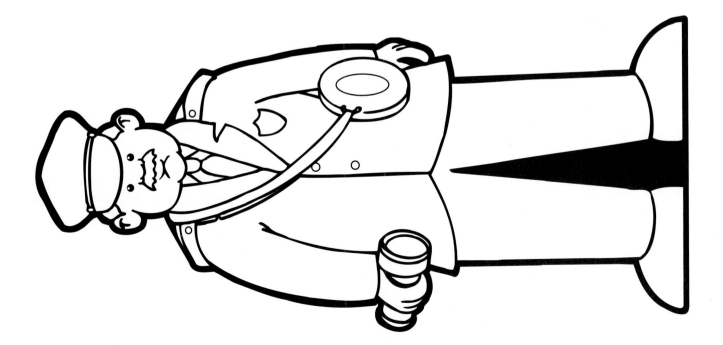

Don't Forget the Bacon!

Written and illustrated by Pat Hutchins

My goodness! How do six farm eggs and a pound of pears become six clothes pegs and a pile of chairs? By changing one word or phoneme at a time on a child's mental shopping list! The rhyming word play at the root of this shopping mishap is sure to tickle your youngsters' funny bones!

Skill: Identify rhyming words.

Teacher Preparation

Literature selection: Preview a copy of *Don't Forget the Bacon!*

Craft:

- Cut one or more kitchen sponges into rectangles that are approximately 1" x 1¹/₂" for students to share. Clip a clothespin to each sponge piece for easy handling.

- Set out yellow and brown tempera paint. Cover students' work area with newspaper.

- Gather the remaining student materials listed below.

- For the literacy link activity described on page 49, list the words shown below on a sheet of chart paper. Make a white construction paper copy of page 51. Cut the picture-word cards apart. If desired, have a volunteer color each card and glue it onto a blank card for durability.

Student Materials

Each student needs the following:
- copy of page 50
- 12" paper plate
- 1¹/₂" x 12" strip of white construction paper
- access to prepared sponges and paint
- access to a stapler
- scissors

Word List		
can	snake	vest
bell	duck	barn
goat	dog	clock
hat	king	flag
bee	car	chick

Begin With a Book

Don't Forget the Bacon!

The boy in this story learns that it's hard to remember a grocery list, especially when there are lots of distractions! Read the book aloud; then prompt a class discussion about the boy's confusion. Point out that it involves rhyming words. Guide students to recall the rhymes in the story, referring to the book as necessary. Then focus on one set of rhyming words—such as *pears, stairs,* and *chairs*—by asking students to identify the sounds that are alike and different. Next, give each student the materials listed on page 48. Have him refer to the directions on page 50 to make a basket for his own rhyme-filled shopping excursion.

Step 1

Continue With a Craft

Handy Shopping Basket

Directions:

1. Have each child sponge-paint rows in an AB pattern across the back of his paper plate.
2. Instruct him to copy the pattern on the paper strip. Allow the plate and strip to dry.
3. Direct the youngster to fold the plate in half and then unfold it slightly and cut along the fold.
4. To make a basket, help him align and staple the plate halves together so the painted pattern faces outward.
5. To make a handle, assist the child in stapling the strip (paint side out) to the basket.

Step 2

Link With a Literacy Skill

A Tisket, a Tasket!

In this rhyme center, written reminders will help your young shoppers avoid the mistakes made in *Don't Forget the Bacon!* Label a center "Class Store" and stock it with the prepared picture-word cards. (To modify the activity for younger students, set out a smaller number of cards and reduced the list of rhyming words shown on page 48.) Display the word list and a supply of blank cards nearby. Invite pairs of students, in turn, to visit the center with their baskets. Ask the students in each twosome to take turns role-playing a shopper and a cashier.

The cashier spreads out the cards in the center so that they can be easily viewed. The shopper selects three words from the posted list and writes each one on a separate card. Then he looks among the picture-word cards for words that rhyme with the ones he has written. When he finds one, he places the two corresponding cards in his basket. After he finds a rhyme for each of his words, he presents the basket to the cashier. The cashier removes the cards, reads them aloud, and returns each confirmed rhyming pair to the basket. At the conclusion of the activity, each youngster uses his basket to take his word cards home.

Step 3

Handy Shopping Basket

Follow the directions.

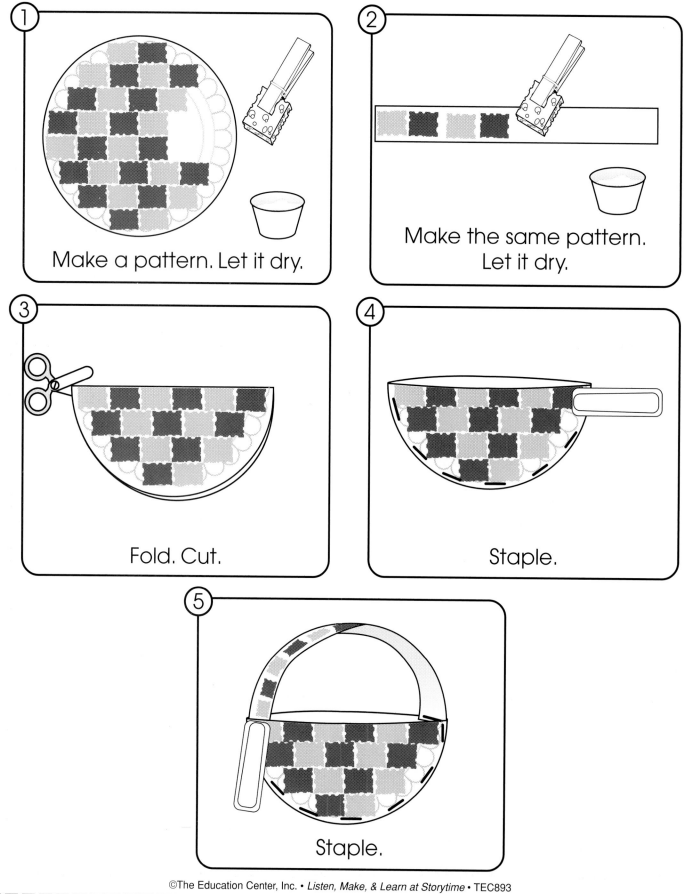

1. Make a pattern. Let it dry.

2. Make the same pattern. Let it dry.

3. Fold. Cut.

4. Staple.

5. Staple.

Note to the teacher: Use with the *Don't Forget the Bacon!* unit that begins on page 48.

fan

star

shell

truck

nest

boat

frog

ring

yarn

cat

sock

cake

bag

stick

tree

Four Famished Foxes and Fosdyke

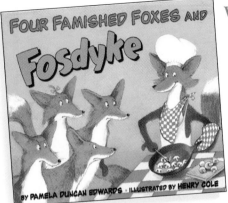

Written by Pamela Duncan Edwards
Illustrated by Henry Cole

Five young foxes are thrilled when their mother goes out of town and they are left to find their own food. Four of the foxes eagerly set their sights on a farmyard feast. The other fox busily prepares French food. Humorous alliterative text describes the results of the foxes' contrasting endeavors and how the four foragers come to realize that "a fox is a fox, whatever the food."

Skills: Explore alliteration.
Identify words that begin with f.

Teacher Preparation

Literature selection: Preview a copy of *Four Famished Foxes and Fosdyke*.

Craft:
- Set out tempera paint in shallow containers. Place a plastic fork by each container.

- Cover students' work area with newspaper for easy cleanup.

- Gather the remaining student materials listed below.

- For the literacy link activity on page 53, obtain a class supply of paper napkins and plastic forks. Also provide access to crayons and glue.

Extension: If desired, make a copy of page 55 for each student to complete at the conclusion of the literacy link activity on page 53.

Student Materials

Each student needs the following:
- copy of page 54
- 9" x 12" sheet of colored construction paper
- tempera paint and a plastic fork
- 6" paper plate
- crayons

Begin With a Book
Four Famished Foxes and Fosdyke

What's on the menu? A fabulous fox story served with a generous helping of alliteration! Show students the book cover and read the title aloud. Confirm that students know the meaning of the word *famished*. To prepare students for additional story vocabulary, do a picture walk, incorporating selected words into the discussion as appropriate. Then read the book aloud. Ask students what they notice about the words that the author used. Guide them to realize that many of them start with *f*. Point out that the illustrations reflect this alliterative element. Challenge students to identify details in the illustrations that begin with *f* as you display each page. To further explore alliteration, distribute the materials listed on page 52. Use the directions below to guide each student in making a fancy placemat for an alliterative feast!

Continue With a Craft
Pretty Painted Placemat

Directions:
1. Instruct each student to dip a plastic fork in the paint. Have her begin at the top left and drag the fork across the paper to make parallel prints.
2. Ask her to repeat the process to create several rows of prints.
3. Direct her to make vertical prints in a similar manner until her paper is covered with a plaidlike design. Allow the paint to dry.
4. To prepare a plate for her placemat, have the youngster color the rim of her paper plate.

Link With a Literacy Skill
Appetite for Alliteration

No doubt Fosdyke and his siblings helped your youngsters develop a taste for alliteration! To serve up more alliteration fun, help students use their placemats and plates to make an eye-catching display. Direct each youngster to write or illustrate on her plate three or more words that begin with *f*. Then give her a paper napkin and a plastic fork. Instruct her to glue the plate, napkin, and fork on her placemat as shown. (If necessary, have her glue the napkin closed so that the project can be easily displayed.) Ask each student to show the class her work and tell them the words that she featured. Then display students' creative place settings on a bulletin board titled "A Fabulous Feast!"

Pretty Painted Placemat

Follow the directions.

1. Dip.

2. Drag the fork to paint lines across.

3. Dip again. Paint more lines.

4. Now paint lines that go up and down. Let dry.

5. Color the rim of the plate.

Note to the teacher: Use with the *Four Famished Foxes and Fosdyke* unit that begins on page 52.

Name _____

Find the Frame!

Cut. Read the words.
Glue to match.
Color.

©The Education Center, Inc. • *Listen, Make, & Learn at Storytime* • TEC893

funny fox	fat fox	fast fox	farm fox	fancy fox

Note to the teacher: Use with the *Four Famished Foxes and Fosdyke* unit that begins on page 52.

55

The Gardener

Written by Sarah Stewart
Illustrated by David Small

Young Lydia Grace has a fondness for gardening, so it's no surprise that she packs some seeds when she travels to live with Uncle Jim during the Great Depression. Soon after her arrival in the city, she hatches a plan to put her gardening skills to use and bring a smile to the face of her cantankerous uncle. Caldecott Honor–winning illustrations and text presented in letter format reveal how Lydia Grace carries out her heartwarming surprise.

Skill: Write a brief letter.

Teacher Preparation

Literature selection: Preview a copy of *The Gardener*. Copy the letter shown below on a sheet of chart paper.

Craft:

- Gather several smooth, clean Styrofoam trays. For each student, cut a 1½-inch Styrofoam square.

- Set out a desired number of washable ink pads in assorted colors.

- Cover students' work area with newspaper for easy cleanup, if desired.

- Gather the remaining student materials listed below.

Student Materials

Each student needs the following:
- copy of pages 58 and 59
- 1½" Styrofoam square
- empty film canister or a large, empty spool
- 5½" x 8½" piece of white paper
- access to washable ink pads
- craft glue
- pencil
- scissors

Dear Students,
    Today we will read a book called The Gardener. It is a story about a girl named Lydia Grace who lives with her uncle for a while. I think you will like the surprise ending!

Sincerely,
Your Teacher

Begin With a Book
The Gardener

Step **1**

Lydia Grace travels far from home, but her loving family is never far from her thoughts! Display the prepared letter and read it aloud. Explain that Lydia Grace lives with her uncle during the Great Depression, a time when people didn't have much money. Invite students to share their ideas about how she might keep in touch with her family at home. Lead them to conclude that she could write letters. As you share the book, ask students to notice how the young girl's letters reveal information about her, her family, and her friends. Then tell students that each of them will follow Lydia Grace's example and put their letter-writing skills to use. To make decorative stationery for this purpose, give each student the materials listed on page 56 and use the steps below.

Continue With a Craft
Special Delivery

Step **2**

Directions:
1. To make a stamp, tell each student to cut away the corners of his Styrofoam square.
2. Have him draw a simple design or picture on the foam.
3. Instruct him to trace his artwork with a pencil, gently pressing down to create grooves.
4. Direct him to glue the blank side of the stamp to the bottom of a film canister or one end of a spool. Let the glue dry.
5. Tell him to use his stamp and the provided ink pads to make a design across the top of the paper.
6. Have him cut out his envelope. Then instruct him to fold the envelope on the dotted lines and glue it as indicated.
7. Ask him to use his stamp to make one print in the lower left-hand corner of the envelope and another print on the envelope flap.

Link With a Literacy Skill
Letter-Perfect Writing

Step **3**

Now that your youngsters have made their own stationery, no doubt they'll be eager to write letters, just like Lydia Grace! Use selected pages of the book to review the format of a friendly letter with students. Then have each youngster use his prepared stationery to write a letter to a chosen friend or family member. Demonstrate how to fold the letter in thirds. After each student folds his completed letter, have him place it inside his envelope. Help him address his envelope for later hand delivery (or have him prepare it at home to be mailed). Now that's a letter-perfect follow-up!

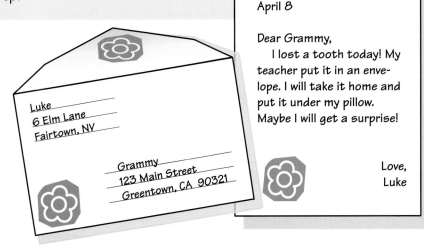

Luke
6 Elm Lane
Fairtown, NV

Grammy
123 Main Street
Greentown, CA 90321

April 8

Dear Grammy,
 I lost a tooth today! My teacher put it in an envelope. I will take it home and put it under my pillow. Maybe I will get a surprise!

Love,
Luke

Special Delivery

Follow the directions.

1. Cut.
2. Draw.
3. Trace.
4. Glue. Let dry.
5. Use the stamp and ink to decorate.
6. Cut.
7. Fold. Glue.
8. Use the stamp and ink to decorate.

Note to the teacher: Use with *The Gardener* unit that begins on page 56.

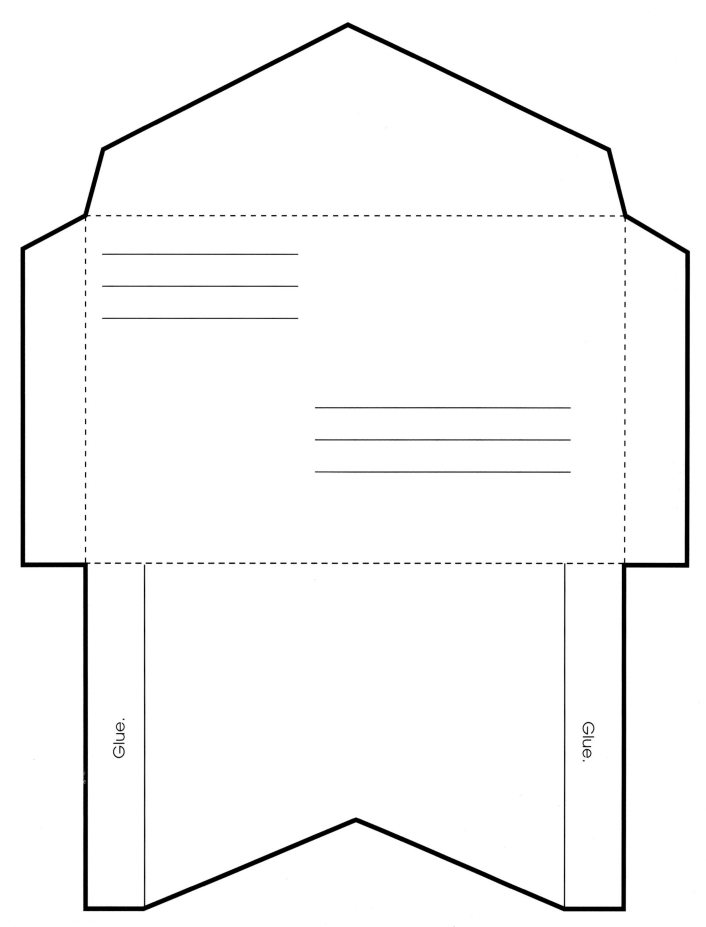

Glue.

Glue.

Goldilocks and the Three Bears

Retold and illustrated by Jan Brett

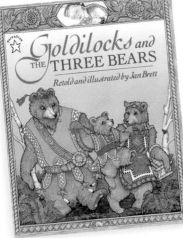

Intricate illustrations bring the adventures of Goldilocks to life in this charming version of a childhood favorite. Each page boasts a border of detailed wood carvings that complement Goldilocks's mischievous exploration of the bears' home. The borders provide glimpses of concurrent scenes and are sure to intrigue keen observers.

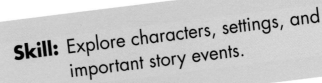

Skill: Explore characters, settings, and important story events.

Teacher Preparation

Literature selection: Preview a copy of *Goldilocks and the Three Bears*.

Craft:

- For each student, cut a wedge from a six-inch paper plate that is slightly less than one-fourth of the plate. Discard the wedge.
- Set out brown tempera paint. Cut one or more kitchen sponges into small pieces for sponge painting. Clip a clothespin to each one for easy handling.
- Cover students' work area with newspaper for easy cleanup.
- Gather the remaining student materials listed below.

Student Materials

Each student needs the following:
- copy of page 62
- white construction paper copy of page 63
- prepared 6" paper plate (See instructions above.)
- brown tempera paint and access to a sponge and clothespin
- small amount of natural raffia that has been cut into 2" lengths
- small amount of dried Spanish moss
- crayons
- scissors
- glue
- brad

Begin With a Book

Goldilocks and the Three Bears

Explore story elements with the three bears and their young intruder! Ask students if they have heard the story of Goldilocks and the three bears. Have a volunteer familiar with the tale identify the characters, setting, and main events in a version she knows. Invite students who have heard other versions to tell how the story elements differ or how they are the same. Next, display and read the cover of the featured book. Ask students to pay particular attention to the characters, settings, and main events as you read the book aloud. Then invite them to share their observations. To further explore story elements, give each student the materials listed on page 60 and help her follow the provided directions to make a character wheel.

Step 1

Continue With a Craft

Character Wheel

Step 2

Directions:
1. Have each student sponge-paint the paper plate brown. Let the paint dry.
2. Instruct her to color and cut out the character wheel. Have her set it aside.
3. Direct her to cut out the windows and glue them on the plate as shown below.
4. Have her glue the raffia to the top of the plate to make a roof.
5. Tell her to glue the moss on either side of the opening to make bushes.
6. Help each student use a brad to secure the paper plate atop her wheel.

Link With a Literacy Skill

Spin a Character!

Step 3

This clue-filled review of *Goldilocks and the Three Bears* puts a spin on story elements! Ask each student to hold her completed character wheel. Then recall a selected story event, using dialogue appropriate for the character. For example, you might say, "Somebody has been sitting in my chair, and has sat the bottom right out of it!" in a tiny voice to give clues for the little, small, wee bear. Tell each student to silently identify the corresponding character by spinning her wheel to the appropriate illustration. Have each youngster hold up her wheel to show you her response. Verify the correct answer. Next, ask a volunteer to identify the setting for the corresponding scene; display the appropriate page in the book. Repeat the process with a desired number of different story events. Then encourage each student to take her character wheel home and use it to retell the story to her family.

Character Wheel

Follow the directions.

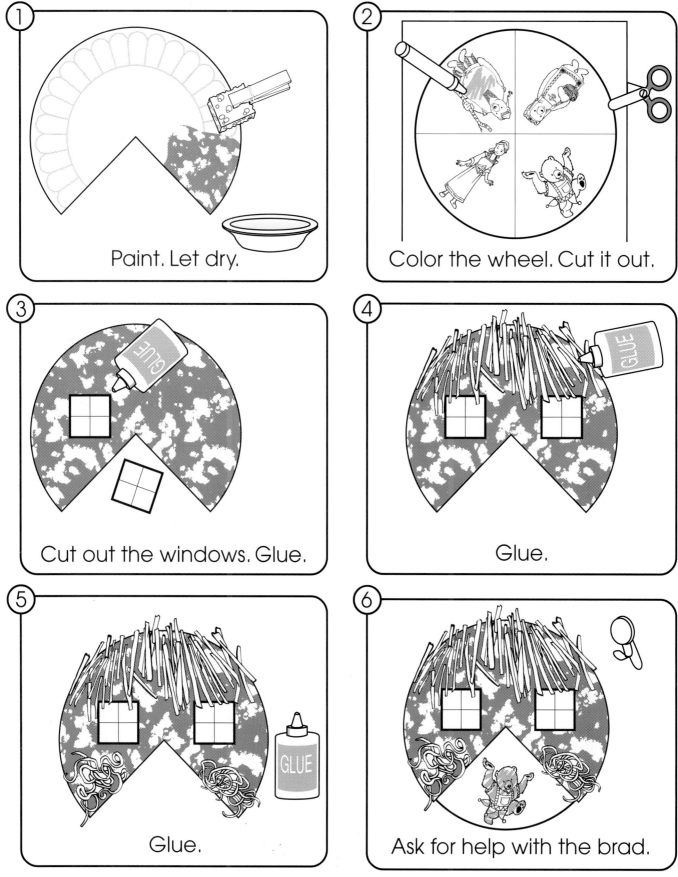

1 Paint. Let dry.

2 Color the wheel. Cut it out.

3 Cut out the windows. Glue.

4 Glue.

5 Glue.

6 Ask for help with the brad.

Note to the teacher: Use with the *Goldilocks and the Three Bears* unit that begins on page 60.

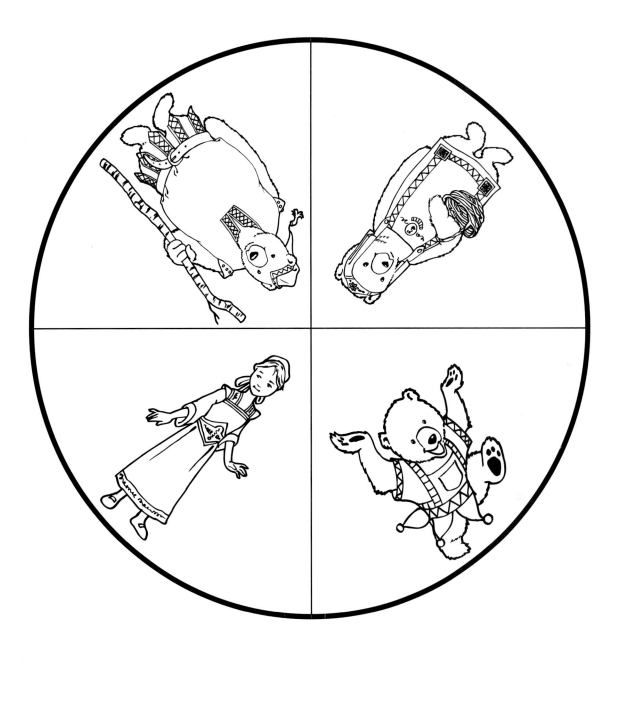

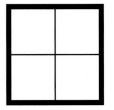 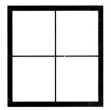

Good-Night, Owl!

Written and illustrated by Pat Hutchins

Owl wants to sleep, but a number of forest critters keep him awake with their incessant chatter. A clever combination of onomatopoeia and patterned text brings the forest sounds to life, prompting young listeners to wonder how Owl will ever get peace and quiet. A surprise ending reveals his response to the frustrating situation.

Skills: Explore story vocabulary. Participate in choral reading.

Teacher Preparation

Literature selection: Preview a copy of *Good-Night, Owl!*

Craft:

• Make a copy of page 67 for each child. Use a craft knife to cut two slits in the tree pattern where indicated.

• Gather the remaining student materials listed below.

Student Materials

Each student needs the following:
• copy of page 66
• prepared copy of page 67 (See instructions above.)
• two 5 mm wiggle eyes
• crayons
• scissors
• glue

Begin With a Book
Good-Night, Owl!

Good night; sleep tight! Ask each student whether he has ever had a difficult time falling asleep. Invite students who have had difficulty to tell the class what kept them awake. Then display the book cover and read the title. Tell students that Owl is having trouble sleeping. Prompt youngsters to predict why Owl can't sleep. Encourage students to listen for the reason as you read the featured book aloud. Then guide students to compare their predictions to the story's actual events. Next, revisit each page with students to review the types of animals and their sounds, as well as any unfamiliar vocabulary. Reread the book, encouraging listeners to chime in with the animal sounds. Then give each student the materials listed on page 64. Have him refer to the illustrated directions as you use the steps below to guide him in making his own tree of sleepless critters.

Continue With a Craft
A Crowded Tree

Directions:
1. Have each student color the patterns.
2. Instruct him to cut out the tree pattern and strips along the bold lines.
3. To assemble the strip, ask him to glue the starling box to the shaded area above the jay.
4. Help him thread the strip through the slits in the tree.
5. Tell him to glue the wiggle eyes on the owl.

Link With a Literacy Skill
Quiet, Please!

"Whooo" can resist the chance to imitate the sounds that keep Owl awake? Not your students! To lead a choral reading of this inviting book, have each student hold his completed tree project and slide the strip until the bee picture can be seen in his tree. Instruct each youngster to point to the word *bee* and read it aloud. Explain that the captioned picture also shows the sound that the bee makes *(buzz)*. Confirm that every student is familiar with the remaining animal names and sounds on the strip. Then, as you slowly reread the story, have each student slide his strip to reveal each animal the first time it is mentioned, and ask him to make the indicated sound. Encourage each student to take his tree project home and use it to tell the noisy story to his family. With this animal chorus, it's no wonder Owl can't sleep!

A Crowded Tree

Follow the directions.

1. Color the tree picture and animals.

2. Cut them out.

3. Glue.

4. Thread.

5. Glue.

Note to the teacher: Use with the *Good-Night, Owl!* unit that begins on page 64.

Good-Night, Owl!

©The Education Center, Inc.

ark — jay

cuckoo — cuckoo

pip — robin

cheep — sparrow

croo — dove

buzz — bee

crunch — squirrel

caw — crow

rat-a-tat — woodpecker

twit-twit — starling

The Great Gracie Chase: Stop That Dog!

Written by Cynthia Rylant
Illustrated by Mark Teague

A little round pooch named Gracie Rose enjoys a quiet, predictable life in a cozy home. But all that changes the day the painters come. Annoyed with the noise and the disruption to her daily routine, Gracie Rose decides to go for a walk. One thing leads to another, and soon everyone, from the painters to a cat, takes part in a hilarious chase across town!

Skill: Recognize cause and effect.

Teacher Preparation

Literature selection: Preview a copy of *The Great Gracie Chase*.

Craft:

• Gather the student materials listed below.

Extension: If desired, make a copy of page 71 for each student to complete at the conclusion of the literacy link activity described on page 69.

Student Materials

Each student needs the following:
• copy of page 70
• white paper lunch bag
• access to a brown washable ink pad
• 2" square of black felt
• 2" square of pink construction paper
• 2" square of aluminum foil
• two 10 mm wiggle eyes
• permanent markers, including black
• glue
• scissors

68

Begin With a Book

The Great Gracie Chase

The noisy arrival of the painters sets off a chain of events, one that Gracie's owners probably never expected! Invite students who have pets or know people who do to tell the class about things the animals like, such as games of fetch or kitty treats. Tell students that you will read aloud a book about a pet who likes a quiet house. Invite students to predict what happens when the pet's house becomes noisy one day. Read the book aloud to check the predictions and then compare them to the actual events. To further explore cause and effect, distribute the materials listed on page 68. Have each child refer to the illustrated directions as you help her make a puppy puppet to use with the literacy link activity below. Bow-wow!

Continue With a Craft

Puppy Puppet

Directions:

1. Direct each student to position her bag with the flap at the top. Have her fold the top corners down to resemble dog ears.
2. Instruct her to draw an oval near the bottom edge of the flap as shown. Ask her to cut the felt to make a nose and glue it on the oval.
3. Direct her to make overlapping fingerprints on part of the flap so that the puppet will resemble Gracie.
4. Have her cut the pink paper into a tongue shape and then glue it under the flap.
5. Ask her to glue on two wiggle eyes.
6. Have her use a marker to draw a collar.
7. Instruct her to cut a circle from the foil, label it with a chosen dog name, and then glue it onto the collar. Invite her to illustrate a ring to connect the tag to the collar.

Link With a Literacy Skill

Noise, Noise, Noise!

There's no doubt about it—Gracie isn't pleased with the noise that the painters cause! To explore other noises and their sources, gather students with their puppets in a circle. Announce a noise-related word such as *beep, crash, hiss,* or *crunch.* Ask each student who knows how the sound might be caused to make his puppet softly bark. Then have volunteers tell the class their ideas. (Be sure to point out that a variety of responses is possible.) Continue in a like manner with a desired number of words. Now that's an idea that makes cause and effect practice tail-waggin' fun!

Puppy Puppet

Follow the directions.

1. Fold.

2. Draw an oval.

3. Cut out a nose. Glue.

4. Make fingerprints.

5. Cut out a tongue. Glue.

6. Glue on two eyes.

7. Draw a collar.

8. Make a circle. Write a name. Glue. Draw to connect the tag.

Spot

Note to the teacher: Use with *The Great Gracie Chase: Stop That Dog!* unit that begins on page 68.

Name_____

Dog Tales

What happens next?
Cut and glue to show your answers.

Bonus Box: Look at the last two pictures. On the back of this sheet, write to tell about them.

©The Education Center, Inc. • *Listen, Make, & Learn at Storytime* • TEC893

Note to the teacher: Use with *The Great Gracie Chase: Stop That Dog!* unit that begins on page 68.

71

Here Comes Henny

Written by Charlotte Pomerantz
Illustrated by Nancy Winslow Parker

HERE COMES HENNY

By Charlotte Pomerantz
Pictures by Nancy Winslow Parker

Henny packs a picnic snicky-snacky for her three chicks—only to have them refuse to eat it and demand something different. After Henny eats the snack herself, the unappreciative chicks realize that they've been too picky. Nonsense words and delightful tongue-twisting text make this book a favorite among children who like to play with words.

Skill: Sort words by -ack and -ick word families.

Teacher Preparation

Literature selection: Preview a copy of *Here Comes Henny*.

Craft:

- For each student, cut three inches from the top of a white paper lunch bag.
- Gather the remaining student materials listed below.

Student Materials

Each student needs the following:
- copy of pages 74 and 75
- prepared white paper lunch bag (See instructions above.)
- two 1" x 6" strips of construction paper
- crayons
- scissors
- glue

Begin With a Book

Here Comes Henny

Henny is packed and ready to go! But where is she headed? Display the book and read the title aloud. Ask students to share their ideas about Henny's destination and what she has in her backpack. Read the first two pages aloud; then pause and invite students to comment on the silly text. Encourage them to listen for other examples of how the author plays with words as you share the rest of the book. At the book's conclusion, ask students to compare their predictions with the story events. Also have students recall the nonsense words and other wordplay that they noticed. Then give each youngster the materials listed on page 72. Help him use the provided directions to make and pack a backpack of his own.

Continue With a Craft

Snick-Snack Backpack

Directions:
1. Have each student color the backpack and cards. Instruct him to cut them out.
2. Ask him to place the white paper bag flap side down on a work surface.
3. Direct him to glue the backpack on the bag. Then have him open and stand the bag.
4. Ask him to fold over both ends of each strip approximately one inch.
5. Have him glue the ends of the strips onto the back of the bag to resemble straps.
6. Instruct him to place the cards in the resulting backpack.

Link With a Literacy Skill

Snicky or Snacky?

The chicks are eager to see what Henny packed in her backpack, and no doubt your youngsters are just as eager to investigate the contents of their backpacks. Lead students in chorally reading the lines on their backpacks. Explain that each youngster will answer the questions with the help of a partner. To prepare students for this task, write "snick" and "snack" on the chalkboard. Prompt a class discussion to compare the words and point out the word endings. Pair students and then have each student remove the cards from his bag, close the bag, and place it faceup. Ask him to stack his cards facedown.

In turn, each student takes the top card in his stack, reads it aloud, and then places it on the corresponding word family box. His partner then says the word, adding a *y* sound to the end of it to imitate Henny and her chicks. After all the cards have been sorted in this manner, each youngster opens his bag and drops his cards inside for easy transport home.

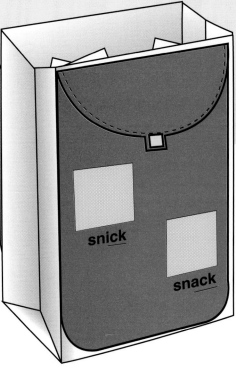

Snick-Snack Backpack

Follow the directions.

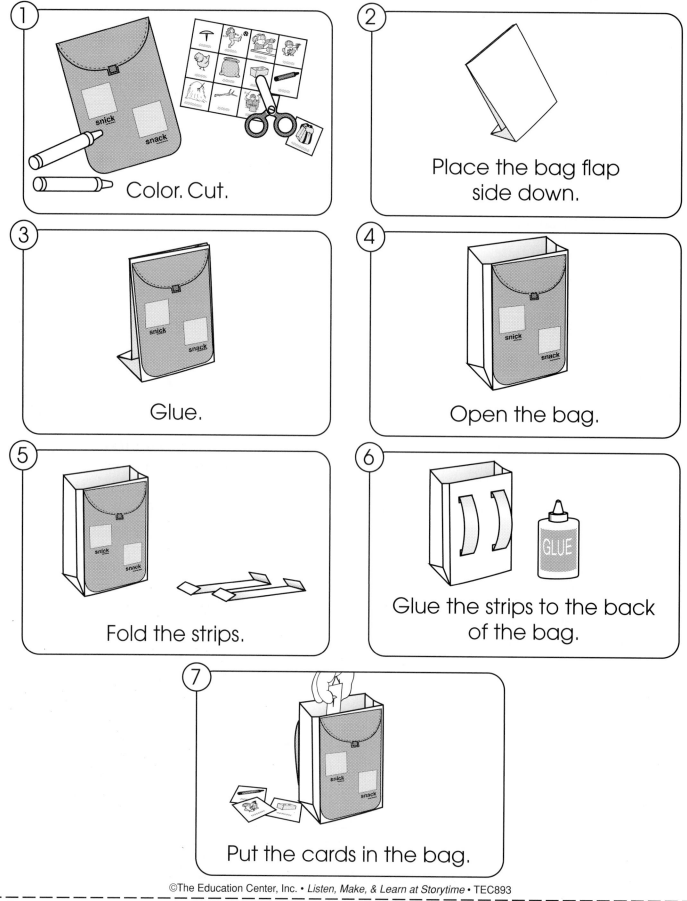

1. Color. Cut.

2. Place the bag flap side down.

3. Glue.

4. Open the bag.

5. Fold the strips.

6. Glue the strips to the back of the bag.

7. Put the cards in the bag.

Note to the teacher: Use with the *Here Comes Henny* unit that begins on page 72.

Patterns

Use with the *Here Comes Henny* unit that begins on page 72.

What words did I pack, pack, pack, pack?
Are they like **snick** or **sn<u>ack</u>?**

sn<u>ack</u>

sn<u>ick</u>

tack	kick	stack	pick
chick	sack	brick	black
haystack	stick	trick	backpack

If You Give a Mouse a Cookie

Written by Laura Joffe Numeroff
Illustrated by Felicia Bond

If you read this book to a child, she'll want to hear it again and again! When a boy gives a mouse a cookie, one thing leads to another, resulting in a very tiring day. Humorous illustrations and grin-inducing cause and effect relationships make this circular story a favorite.

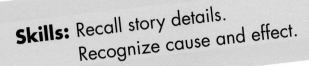

Skills: Recall story details.
Recognize cause and effect.

Teacher Preparation

Literature selection: Preview a copy of *If You Give a Mouse a Cookie.*

Craft:

• Cut out a copy of the window pattern on page 79. For each student, cut an 8½" circle from tagboard. Use the window pattern to make two wedge-shaped cuts in it as shown.

• Cover students' work area with newspaper. Set out damp paper towels for easy cleanup, if desired.

• Set out small, shallow containers of washable black tempera paint.

• Gather the remaining student materials listed below.

Student Materials

Each student needs the following:
• copy of page 78
• white construction paper copy of page 79
• prepared tagboard circle (See instructions above.)
• brown fingerpaint
• black tempera paint
• scissors
• 2 brads

Begin With a Book

If You Give a Mouse a Cookie

From cookies and milk to milk and cookies, this literature-based exploration of cause and effect is sure to hit the spot! Display the book cover and read the title aloud. Encourage youngsters to predict what happens when the mouse is given a cookie. Then read the book aloud. Invite students to compare their predictions with the story events. Next, do a picture walk through the book, prompting volunteers to recall the cause and effect relationships depicted. To serve up more practice with this concept, give each student the materials listed on page 76 and guide her to make a jumbo painted cookie as described below.

Continue With a Craft

Cookie Time!

Directions:
1. Have each student fingerpaint her tagboard circle.
2. Instruct her to use black paint to make fingerprints on the resulting cookie so that they resemble chocolate chips. Allow the paint to dry for several hours.
3. Direct the child to cut out the wheel patterns on her copy of page 79. (She may discard the window pattern.)
4. Help her use a brad to attach Wheel A to the cookie so that each illustration, in turn, can be seen through the left window when the wheel is rotated. Help her attach Wheel B to the right-hand side of the cookie in a like manner.

Link With a Literacy Skill

What Next?

If your students make the tempting cookie project described above, no doubt they'll be eager to use it in a review of story details! Gather students in a circle with their completed projects. Announce the first cause listed below and have each student turn her Wheel A to show the corresponding picture. Next, encourage each student to silently recall what happens next in the story and then turn Wheel B to reveal the answer. Ask each student to hold up her project to show you. Scan students' raised projects for accuracy and select a volunteer to explain the correct answer. Repeat the process with the remaining cause and effect pairs listed below.

For additional reinforcement, pair students. Have each student in a twosome take turns showing a cause and asking her partner to show the corresponding effect. Conclude the activity with a class snack of chocolate chip cookies (and perhaps some milk to go with it!).

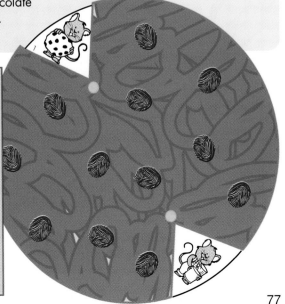

Cause	Effect
1. A mouse eats a cookie.	He gets thirsty and asks for milk.
2. The mouse has a milk mustache.	He wipes his face with a napkin.
3. The floor is messy.	The mouse sweeps the floor.
4. The mouse washes the floor.	He gets tired.
5. The mouse draws a picture.	He wants to tape it to the refrigerator.

Cookie Time!

Follow the directions.

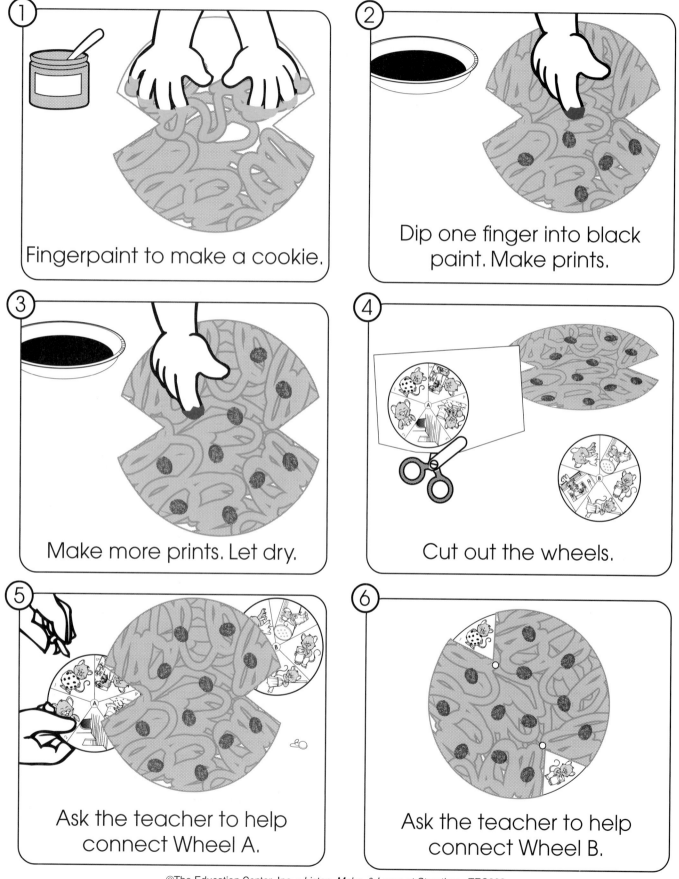

1. Fingerpaint to make a cookie.

2. Dip one finger into black paint. Make prints.

3. Make more prints. Let dry.

4. Cut out the wheels.

5. Ask the teacher to help connect Wheel A.

6. Ask the teacher to help connect Wheel B.

Note to the teacher: Use with the *If You Give a Mouse a Cookie* unit that begins on page 76.

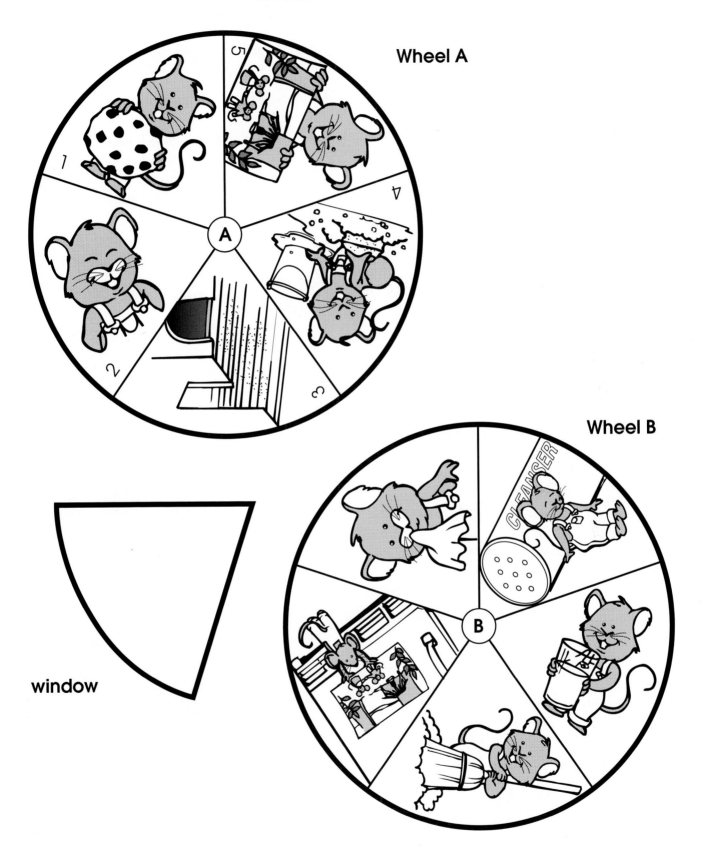

Wheel A

Wheel B

window

In Enzo's Splendid Gardens

Written and illustrated by Patricia Polacco

A bee, a boy, and a book set off a hilarious chain of events in Enzo's splendid gardens! Cumulative rhyming text and humorous illustrations capture the series of mishaps that disrupt an outdoor restaurant.

Skills: Recall story details.
Recognize cause and effect.

Teacher Preparation

Literature selection: Preview a copy of *In Enzo's Splendid Gardens*.

Craft:

• Cut out an eight-inch yellow construction paper circle for each student. Make one copy of the wedge pattern on page 83 and then cut it out. Trace it on each circle as shown.

• Gather the remaining student materials listed below.

Student Materials

Each student needs the following:
• copy of pages 82 and 83
• prepared 8" yellow construction paper circle (See instructions above.)
• 5" yellow construction paper circle
• two ¹/₂" x 5" black construction paper strips
• two 2" x 6" pieces of waxed paper
• brad
• black crayon
• scissors
• glue

Step 1

Begin With a Book

In Enzo's Splendid Gardens

Each turn of events in this comical story will have your students abuzz with anticipation! Stand several dominoes close together in a line. Have students predict what will happen if the first domino is knocked over. Then ask a volunteer to gently tap it. Explain that the result is a chain reaction. Tell students that the events in the featured book reflect a domino effect.

Read the book aloud. Use the illustrations to review how one event causes the next. Then give each youngster the materials listed on page 80. Have him refer to the illustrated steps as you guide him in making a concrete reminder of the unsuspecting insect at the root of the story's chaos.

Step 2

Continue With a Craft

Busy Story Bee

Directions:

1. Have each student color black stripes on the large circle to resemble a bee's body. Instruct him to cut out the indicated wedge.
2. Ask him to glue together the small and large circles as shown below.
3. Have him draw a face on the small circle.
4. Direct him to accordion-fold the paper strips to make antennae. Ask him to glue them to the back of the bee's head.
5. Instruct him to round one short end of each waxed paper rectangle to make wings.
6. Ask him to pinch the straight end of each wing and then glue the wings onto the bee.
7. Instruct him to cut out the provided wheel pattern. (He may discard the wedge pattern.)
8. Help him use a brad to attach the wheel pattern to the bee.

Step 3

Link With a Literacy Skill

Then What Happened?

Who would have guessed that watching a bee could have caused such a commotion? Have students use their bee projects to explore how the chaotic events unfolded. Ask each youngster to turn his wheel so that the starred section is visible. Invite a volunteer to read the sentence aloud. Encourage students to recall what happened in the story as a result of the bee landing on the tree. To check the answer, ask each youngster to turn his wheel clockwise to the next section. Have a student read the newly revealed sentence aloud. Ask students to recall the effect of this action; then check their response as before. Continue in this manner with the remaining sections. Then encourage each youngster to take his project home and use it to retell the "un-bee-lievable" tale to his family!

A bee lands.

81

Busy Story Bee

Follow the directions.

1. Color stripes. Cut.

2. Glue. Draw a face.

3. Fold back and forth. Glue.

4. Cut to make wings.

5. Pinch. Glue.

6. Cut.

7. Connect.

Note to the teacher: Use with the *In Enzo's Splendid Gardens* unit that begins on page 80.

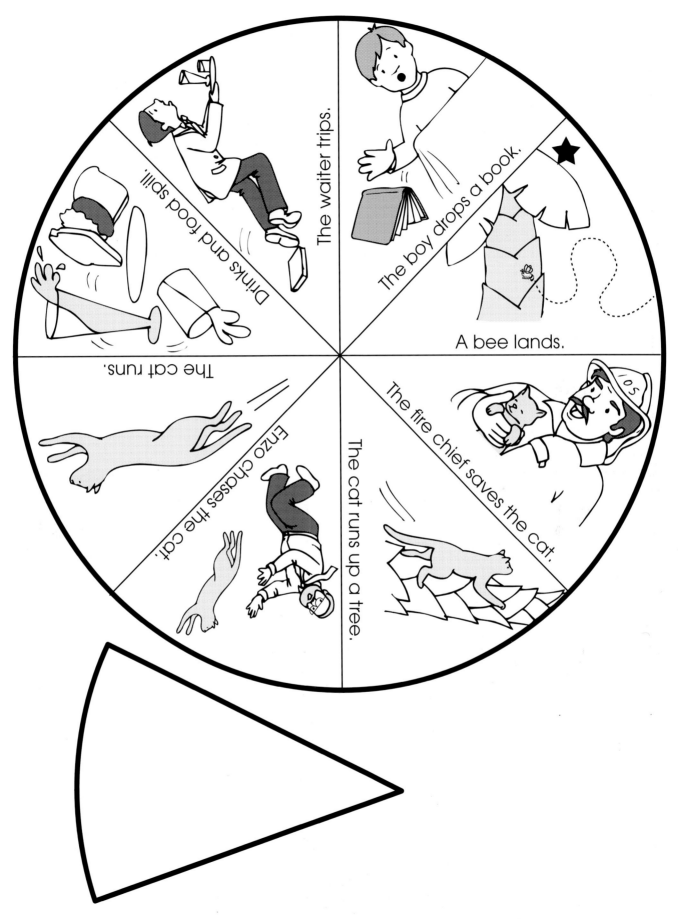

In the Small, Small Pond

Written and illustrated by Denise Fleming

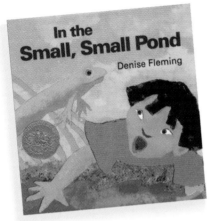

A lot happens in a small, small pond! From the tadpoles that wiggle and jiggle in the spring to the frogs that sleep in the winter, a variety of critters make the pond a busy place! Award-winning illustrations created with handmade paper complement the simple, rhyming text that bounces across the pages.

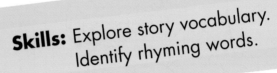

Skills: Explore story vocabulary. Identify rhyming words.

Teacher Preparation

Literature selection: Preview a copy of *In the Small, Small Pond*. List several verbs from the story on a blank card for later reference.

Craft:

• Cover students' work area with newspaper for easy cleanup. Set out blue fingerpaint and paper towels.

• Set out a container of sand and place a plastic spoon in it.

• Gather the remaining student materials listed below.

Student Materials

Each student needs the following:

• copy of pages 86 and 87
• 9" paper plate
• blue fingerpaint
• small amount of green cellophane grass
• a few spoonfuls of sand
• three $1\frac{1}{2}$" squares of white tissue paper
• resealable plastic sandwich bag
• crayons
• scissors
• glue

Begin With a Book

In the Small, Small Pond

Step 1

Use this action-packed book to take students on a vocabulary-boosting trip to the pond! Have students stand in a circle. Announce a verb that you listed on the card, and ask students to pantomime the corresponding action. Invite them to brainstorm a few pond animals that might move in this way. Continue with the remaining listed verbs; then seat students for storytime. Next, explain that the words students acted out are in the featured book. Encourage students to listen for the words as you read the story aloud. Then give each youngster the materials listed on page 84. Have her follow the illustrated steps as you use the directions below to help her make a busy pond.

Continue With a Craft

Pretend Pond

Step 2

Directions:
1. Direct each student to fingerpaint the front of her plate to resemble a pond. Let the paint dry.
2. Have the youngster color the patterns and then cut them out. Ask her to cut out the word cards and store them in the bag.
3. Instruct her to squeeze glue along the fluted portion of the plate. Have her sprinkle sand on the glue and then shake off the excess.
4. Instruct her to glue cellophane grass along the outer portion of the plate.
5. Have her glue the frog, fish, and tadpole patterns on the pond.
6. Ask her to pinch each tissue paper square to make a water lily and then glue it on the pond.
7. Instruct her to fold back the bottom of the turtle and duck patterns. Have her glue the patterns near the edge of the pond so that they stand.

Link With a Literacy Skill

"Pond-ering" Rhymes

Step 3

What's in your students' small, small ponds? Lots of rhyming fun! Reread selected pages from the book and guide students to notice the rhyming words. Next, pair students and ask partners to alternate turns. To take a turn, a student removes a card from her bag and reads the words aloud. If the words rhyme, she places the card on her pond. If they do not, she places the card beside the pond. Play continues until every card has been sorted in this manner. Check students' work; then have each youngster return her cards to her bag. Encourage her to repeat the activity at home for more "pond-errific" practice with rhymes!

Pretend Pond

Follow the directions.

1. Paint. Let dry.

2. Color.

3. Cut out. Put the word cards in the bag.

4. Squeeze glue. Sprinkle sand. Shake.

5. Glue on grass.

6. Glue on the frog and fish. Glue on the tadpole.

7. Pinch. Glue.

8. Fold. Glue.

Note to the teacher: Use with the *In the Small, Small Pond* unit that begins on page 84.

| duck truck | land little | frog red | bell shell | duck green |
| shell big | log frog | fish dish | fish wet | sand land |

Jesse Bear, What Will You Wear?

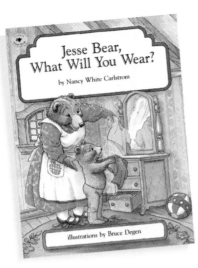

Written by Nancy White Carlstrom
Illustrated by Bruce Degen

What will you find in this book? Rhythm and rhyme and a rollicking good time—that's what you'll find in this book! Jesse Bear's creative (and catchy!) descriptions of his outfits provide an entertaining look at his activities one warm, sunny day.

Skill: Identify rhyming words.

Teacher Preparation

Literature selection: Preview a copy of *Jesse Bear, What Will You Wear?*

Craft:
• Make a tagboard copy of page 91. Cut out the T-shirt patterns to make templates for students to share. Prepare additional templates, if desired.

• Gather the remaining student materials listed below.

Student Materials

Each student needs the following:
• copy of page 90
• old-fashioned clothespin
• access to a brown or tan marker
• 2 brown 10 mm pom-poms
• two 7 mm wiggle eyes
• black 5 mm pom-pom
• access to an extra-fine black marker
• access to a T-shirt template
• two 4" craft-foam squares
• glue
• pencil
• scissors

Begin With a Book

Jesse Bear, What Will You Wear?

Morning, noon, or night, Jesse Bear always has just the right outfit to wear! Ask students whether they help choose the clothes they wear, and if so, what influences their decisions. After several youngsters respond, tell the class that the featured book is about a bear who chooses different outfits throughout one day. Read the book aloud; then lead a class discussion to review Jesse Bear's clothing choices. Reread the book, pausing at selected rhyming words to let students chime in. Next, distribute the materials listed on page 88. Have each child refer to the illustrated directions as you use the steps below to guide him in making a bare bear to dress.

Continue With a Craft

Bear Buddy

Directions:
1. Have each student use a brown marker to color his clothespin from the top to the second indentation. Then instruct him to write his name on one prong.
2. Have him turn the clothespin over so that his name is on the back. Ask him to glue the brown pom-poms to the top of the clothespin to resemble ears.
3. Direct the child to glue the wiggle eyes and black pom-pom to the clothespin as shown below.
4. Instruct the child to use the black marker to draw a mouth on the clothespin.
5. Ask him to trace the shirt template on each craft-foam square and then cut out the tracings.

Link With a Literacy Skill

Bear Wear

Have students dress their bear buddies with shirts inspired by Jesse Bear's rhymes! Give each student a blank card that has been programmed with a different rhyming word pair. Confirm that he is familiar with the words. Have the youngster use a permanent marker to copy each word on a separate shirt cutout. Then gather students in a circle with their bear buddies and programmed shirts.

Randomly select a student. Lead the rest of the class in asking him the following questions: "[Student's name] Bear, what will you wear? What will you wear tomorrow?" Have the youngster use the words on his shirts to complete the answer: "My shirt that says _____ and my shirt that says _____. _____ and _____ tomorrow!" Then ask him to "dress" his bear by clipping the shirts between the prongs. Continue around the circle until every youngster has told the class what his bear will wear.

Bear Buddy

Follow the directions.

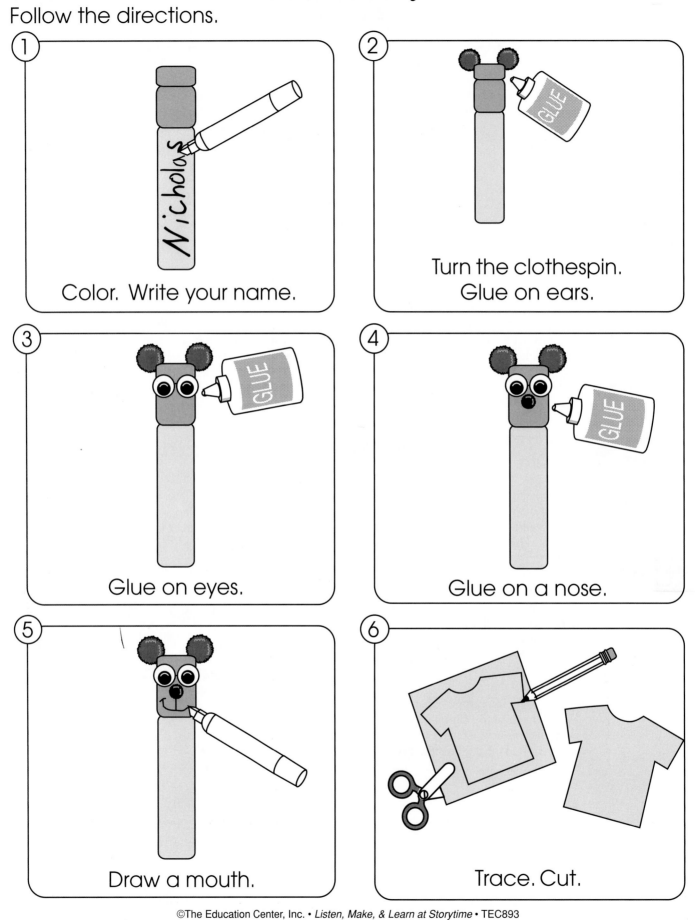

1. Color. Write your name.

2. Turn the clothespin. Glue on ears.

3. Glue on eyes.

4. Glue on a nose.

5. Draw a mouth.

6. Trace. Cut.

Note to the teacher: Use with the *Jesse Bear, What Will You Wear?* unit that begins on page 88.

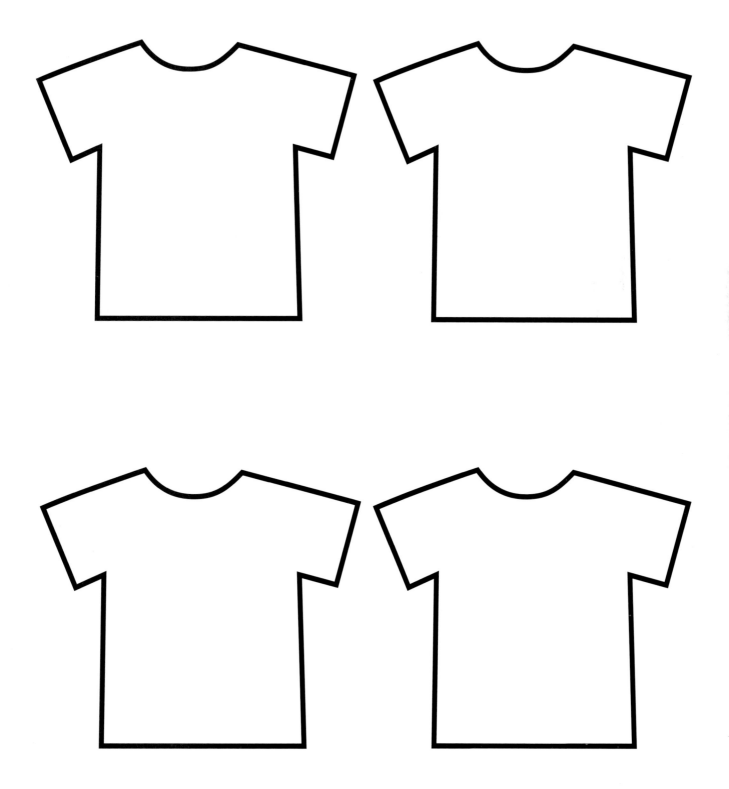

Joseph Had a Little Overcoat

Written and illustrated by Simms Taback

Joseph has a knack for making something new from something old. He is so resourceful, he can even create something out of nothing! Based on a Yiddish folk song, his tale is captured in this award-winning book and presented on die-cut pages illustrated with multimedia collages.

Skill: Use illustrations to tell a story in correct sequence.

Teacher Preparation

Literature selection: Preview a copy of *Joseph Had a Little Overcoat*.

Craft:
• Gather the student materials listed below.

Student Materials

Each student needs the following:
• copy of page 94
• white construction paper copy of page 95
• marker
• pencil
• crayons
• scissors
• access to a stapler

Begin With a Book

Joseph Had a Little Overcoat

Bring the saying "waste not, want not" to life with this tale of ingenuity! In advance, show a selected worn-out article of clothing to students. Explain that you don't want to throw the clothing away, but you don't want to wear it in this condition. Ask students to brainstorm new uses for it. Then tell them that the main character in *Joseph Had a Little Overcoat* has a knack for recycling clothing. Encourage them to listen for his recycling ideas as you read the book aloud.

At the book's conclusion, use the illustrations to help students recall in sequence each item that Joseph creates from the coat. Guide them to realize that each item is smaller than the previous one. Then give each student the materials listed on page 92. Have her refer to the illustrated directions as you use the steps below to help her show how another worn-out coat is put to good use.

Step 1

Continue With a Craft

A Little Coat Booklet

Step 2

Directions:
1. Have each student write her name where indicated on the large pattern. Then have her illustrate her face and hair in the provided space.
2. Instruct her to use a marker to color the patch on the pants. Have her use the same marker to color each heavily outlined article of clothing on the remaining patterns.
3. Direct her to use crayons to finish coloring the patterns.
4. Have her cut out the patterns.
5. Tell her to stack the small patterns in sequence by the size of the heavily outlined items so that the largest item is on top. Ask her to staple the stack onto the large pattern where indicated.

Link With a Literacy Skill

Stories to Tell

Step 3

When it comes to storytelling practice, this story innovation is a perfect fit! Reread the featured book, inviting students to chime in with the predictable text. Then use a volunteer's completed booklet to demonstrate how to use the provided format to tell a story similar to *Joseph Had a Little Overcoat*. Next, pair students. In turn, have each student "read" her booklet to her partner as demonstrated. Then encourage each youngster to take her booklet home and share it with her family. What a fun way to dress up literacy skill reinforcement!

Storytelling Format

[Student's name] had a little [article of clothing]. It got old and worn. So she made a [article of clothing] out of it and [verb phrase].

93

A Little Coat Booklet

Follow the directions.

1 Write your name. Draw your face and hair. Color.

2 Use a marker to color the patch.

3 Use the same marker. Color the coat, vest, belt, and hanky.

4 Use crayons to color the rest.

5 Cut.

6 Stack the pages in order. Staple.

Patterns

Use with the *Joseph Had a Little Overcoat* unit that begins on page 92.

_____'s
Little Overcoat

©The Education Center, Inc.

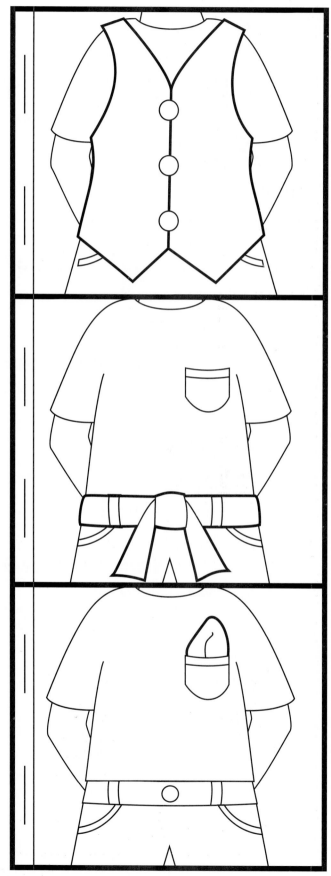

Katy No-Pocket

Written by Emmy Payne
Illustrated by H. A. Rey

How does a pocketless mother kangaroo carry her baby? That's what Katy Kangaroo needs to know! Katy searches high and low for the answer, but to no avail. That is, until her search takes her to the city, where she meets a kind tool-carrying man.

Skill: Apply letter-sound correspondences.

Teacher Preparation

Literature selection: Preview a copy of *Katy No-Pocket*.

Craft:

• Gather the student materials listed below.

• Make eight construction paper copies of the pocket on page 99 for the literacy link on the following page. Cut out the pockets and program one for each of the following letters: *b, c, f, l, m, p, r, t.*

Student Materials

Each student needs the following:
• brown construction paper copy of the kangaroo on page 99
• 2 construction paper copies of the pocket on page 99
• jumbo craft stick
• button
• pencil
• scissors
• glue
• tape

Begin With a Book
Katy No-Pocket

Hop right into creative problem solving with this classic picture book! Display the book cover and read the title aloud. Ask students to use the title and illustration to help them predict who Katy is and what problem she has. Lead them to conclude that Katy is a kangaroo who doesn't have a pocket like other kangaroos do. Have students brainstorm ways that Katy might carry her baby; then read the book aloud. At the conclusion of the book, revisit students' predictions and compare them with Katy's solution. Next, distribute the materials listed on page 96. Ask each youngster to refer to the illustrated steps as you use the directions below to help him make a pocket that's just right for holding a Freddy puppet.

Continue With a Craft
Freddy's Pocket

Directions:
1. Have each student cut out the kangaroo and pockets.
2. Direct him to place one pocket facedown. Have him center the craft stick on the lower half of the pocket. Help him draw a line on the pocket on each side of the stick. Then ask him to put the craft stick aside.
3. Tell him to apply a thin line of glue along the edge of the pocket from each line to the nearest corner. Have him align the second pocket atop the first one and gently rub it to secure it in place.
4. Direct him to glue a button on the pocket flap.
5. Have him tape the craft stick to the back of the kangaroo to make a handle.
6. Instruct him to insert the handle through the pocket openings.

Link With a Literacy Skill
Pop-Up Freddy

Invite students to hop into letter-sound fun with their Freddy puppets! Display the lettered pockets that you prepared earlier, making sure that each letter is easily visible. Ask each student to adjust his puppet and pocket to conceal Freddy. Name an animal listed on this page. If a student knows the initial letter of the word, have him "pop" Freddy up from the pocket. Ask a student who signaled with his puppet as described to come to the pocket display. Have him repeat the name of the animal, point to the corresponding letter, name it, and then say its sound. After the youngster returns to his seat, continue until every programmed letter has been explored in this manner.

Animals	
cow	monkey
lion	bird
rabbit	turtle
fish	pig

Freddy's Pocket

Follow the directions.

1 Cut out the kangaroo and pockets.

2 Place the stick on the back of a pocket. Draw two lines.

3 Move the stick. Glue.

4 Glue on a button.

5 Tape to make a puppet.

6 Put the puppet in the pocket.

Note to the teacher: Use with the *Katy No-Pocket* unit that begins on page 96.

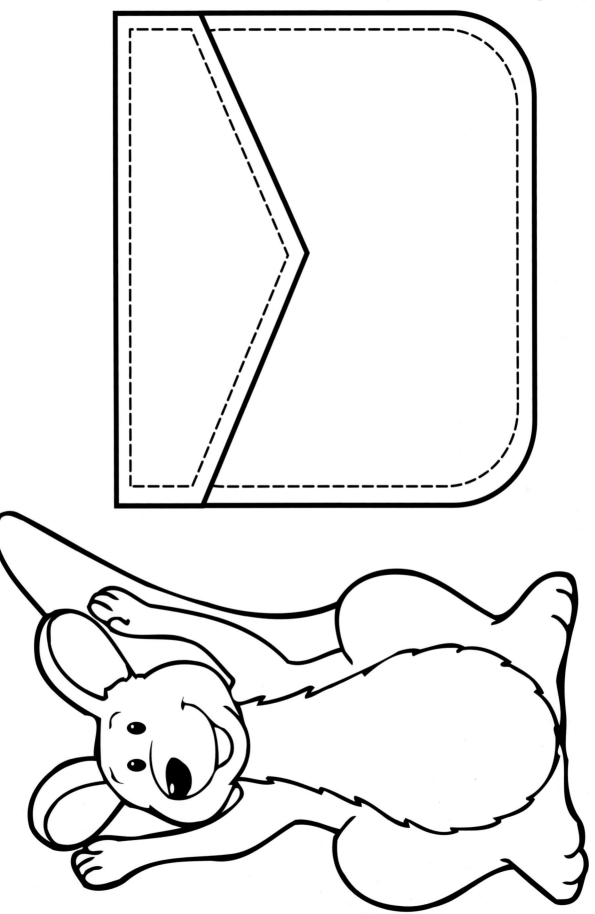

Leo the Late Bloomer

Written by Robert Kraus
Illustrated by José Aruego

Poor Leo! He can't do many of the things that other animals his age can do. Leo's a late bloomer. Then suddenly, when he and his family least expect it, Leo blooms! He can read, write, draw, eat neatly, and speak in complete sentences. Young listeners will readily relate to the challenges of growing up and the joy Leo feels as a result of his accomplishments. Hip, hip, hooray for Leo!

Skill: Apply letter-sound correspondences.

Teacher Preparation

Literature selection: Preview a copy of *Leo the Late Bloomer*.

Craft:

• Gather the student materials listed below.

Student Materials

Each student needs the following:
• copy of page 102
• orange construction paper copy of page 103
• brown paper lunch bag
• two 15 mm wiggle eyes
• 1" x 9" black construction paper strip
• scissors
• glue
• access to a stapler

Begin With a Book

Leo the Late Bloomer

It takes time to grow up! And that's exactly what Leo discovers in this heartwarming story. Show youngsters the book cover and read the title aloud. Ask students to share their ideas about why Leo is called a late bloomer. Guide students to understand that the word *bloom* means to mature or grow and that Leo is taking a little longer than expected to grow up. To further students' understanding, prompt a class discussion about tasks that students couldn't do when they were younger but can do now. Read the book aloud; then distribute the materials listed on page 100. Ask each youngster to refer to the illustrated steps as you use the directions below to help her create a Leo look-alike.

Continue With a Craft

Lovable Leo

Directions:
1. Instruct each child to cut out the patterns.
2. Direct her to glue Leo's head near the top of her bag.
3. Have her glue on the wiggle eyes. Then have her glue one paw on either side of the front panel.
4. Tell her to open the bag and then glue both feet to the bottom of the bag as shown below.
5. Ask her to glue Leo's tail to the back of the bag.
6. Help her staple the construction paper strip to the bag to make a handle.

Link With a Literacy Skill

Letters and Leo

No doubt knowing letters and their sounds helped Leo learn to read! To reinforce what your youngsters know about letters, program a class supply of blank cards, each with a different letter. (If desired, make multiple cards for high-frequency letters to substitute for less common letters.) Place a card in each child's Leo bag. Add a note asking parents to help their youngster find a small object that begins with the assigned letter. Request that they put it in the bag along with the letter card to be returned to school the next day.

When the bags have been returned, divide the class into small groups. In each group, have one student show her object and tell its name. Challenge her group members to identify the corresponding initial letter. Ask the student to hold up the card to check the responses. Repeat this process until every student has shared the item in her bag. Leo would be proud!

Lovable Leo

Follow the directions.

1   Cut.

2   Glue the head.

3   Glue the eyes.

4   Glue the paws. Open the bag. Glue the feet.

5   Glue the tail.

6   Ask your teacher to help you staple.

Note to the teacher: Use with the *Leo the Late Bloomer* unit that begins on page 100.

head

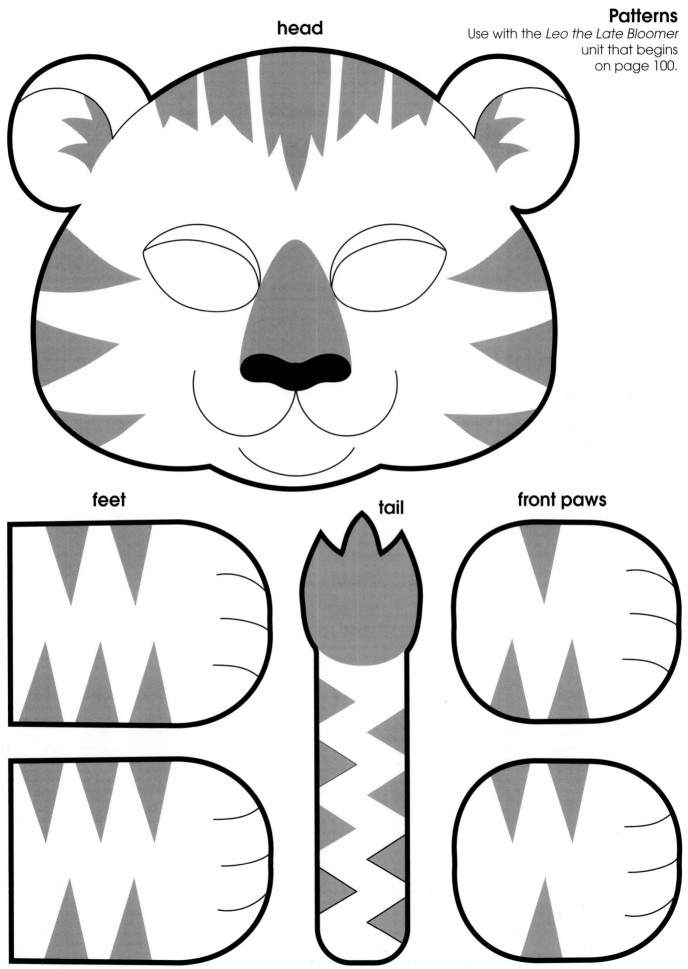

feet

tail

front paws

The Library Dragon

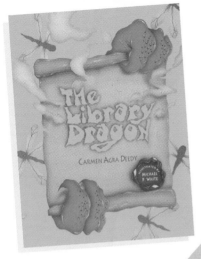

Written by Carmen Agra Deedy
Illustrated by Michael P. White

Miss Lotta Scales is not like other school librarians—she's a fire-breathing dragon whose mission is to protect books from children. But when a young student reads a library book aloud, the fiery librarian's heart softens and she realizes the value of sharing books.

Skills: Identify proper book care behaviors.
Recognize the consonant blend dr.

Teacher Preparation

Literature selection: Preview a copy of *The Library Dragon.*

Craft:

- Gather the student materials listed below.
- For the literacy link activity described on the following page, make a word card for each of the following: *drag, dragon, drain, draw, dream, dress, drill, drink, drive, drop, drum, dry*. Program each of several cards with familiar words that do not have the initial blend *dr*. Scramble all of the cards and place them in a basket. Gather a class supply of blank 3" x 5" cards.

Student Materials

Each student needs the following:
- copy of page 106
- white construction paper copy of page 107
- 6" x 9" sheet of colored construction paper
- several 1" squares of green tissue paper
- plastic spoon
- small sequins
- crayons
- glue
- scissors

Begin With a Book

The Library Dragon

Fire up a class discussion about proper book care! Tell students that the featured book is about a library dragon. Ask them to use what they know about dragons to predict how a library dragon would act. Encourage the youngsters to check their predictions as you read the book aloud. Then have them compare and contrast the library dragon's idea of proper book care with class or school library guidelines. Next, explain that each student will make a dragon that resembles the fiery librarian. Give each youngster the materials listed on page 104. Have him refer to the illustrated steps as you use the directions below to help him complete his project.

Continue With a Craft

Word Dragon

1. Have each student color his patterns and then cut them out.
2. Instruct him to glue the patterns to the construction paper as shown below.
3. Direct him to wrap a tissue paper square around the end of the spoon handle and then slide it off. Ask him to glue the tissue paper onto his dragon to resemble a scale. Have him repeat the process with the remaining tissue paper squares.
4. Instruct him to glue sequins along the edges of the eyeglasses.

Link With a Literacy Skill

On the Lookout for Blends

Miss Scales fiercely guards library books, but your students' dragons will guard *dr* words instead! Draw a large T-chart on the chalkboard and title it "Dragon." Label one column "Yes" and one column "No." Invite a student to read the chart title aloud and underline the first two letters. Explain that the letters work together to make a blend. Have a volunteer remove a word card from the prepared basket, read the word aloud, and then state whether it begins with the blend *dr.* Ask him to use a loop of tape to place the card in the corresponding column. Continue with the remaining cards in a like manner.

Give each youngster a blank index card to complete his dragon project. Ask him to write three or four chosen *dr* words on it and then use a crayon to underline the featured blend in each word. Direct him to glue his writing onto his project as illustrated. Display students' work on a bulletin board along with a poster labeled as shown to create a red-hot reading reference!

The Library Dragon learned that reading is fun. Help her read each word, one by one!

dragon
drop   drum
dream

105

Word Dragon

Follow the directions.

1. Color. Cut out.

2. Glue.

3. Wrap a tissue paper square around the spoon. Slide it off.

4. Glue the tissue paper to look like a scale.

5. Make and glue more scales.

6. Glue.

Note to the teacher: Use with *The Library Dragon* unit that begins on page 104.

Little Blue and Little Yellow

Retold and illustrated by Leo Lionni

Little blue and little yellow are the best of friends! They are so happy to see each other one day that they hug, becoming green. The color change results in confusion, but the misunderstandings are soon resolved. This seemingly simple story, complemented by torn-paper illustrations, provides a tale of friendship and acceptance that can be enjoyed on many levels.

Skills: Label an illustration.
Dictate or write an appropriate caption.

Teacher Preparation

Literature selection: Preview a copy of *Little Blue and Little Yellow.* Use a sticky note to mark the two-page spread that illustrates the games Hide-and-Seek and Ring-a-Ring-O' Roses.

Craft:

• Gather the student materials listed below.

Extension: If desired, make a copy of page 111 for each student to complete at the conclusion of the literacy link activity described on page 109.

Student Materials

Each student needs the following:
• copy of page 110
• 5" blue construction paper square
• 5" yellow construction paper square
• 12" x 18" sheet of white construction paper
• assorted construction paper scraps
• pencil
• crayons
• glue

Begin With a Book
Little Blue and Little Yellow

Little blue and little yellow are two circles. They are also best friends who enjoy playing together. Before reading about the circles' playtime activities, ask students how they like to spend their own free time. List their responses on a sheet of chart paper. As you read the book aloud, encourage students to listen carefully to find out what free-time activities little blue and little yellow enjoy. Then ask youngsters to share their observations.

Next, revisit with students the previously marked pages that illustrate Hide-and-Seek and Ring-a-Ring-O' Roses. Comment that just as the circles like to play these games, many children do too. Ask students if they think little blue and little yellow would enjoy the games and activities that the class listed. Encourage discussion to explore students' answers. Then distribute the materials listed on page 108. Have each child refer to the illustrated directions as you guide her in illustrating more playtime adventures for little blue and little yellow.

Step 1

Continue With a Craft
Playtime Picture

Step 2

Directions:
1. Instruct each child to place the white sheet of paper horizontally on her work surface. Have her fold up the bottom edge approximately two inches. Then have her unfold it and trace the crease. Explain that her illustration should not go below the line.
2. Ask her to tear the squares into two circles.
3. Have her choose a game or activity to illustrate, referring to the list if necessary.
4. To illustrate little blue and little yellow participating in the chosen game or activity, ask the student to glue the circles on the paper. Then have her use crayons, additional torn-paper scraps, and glue to complete her picture.
5. Ask her to label the picture.

Link With a Literacy Skill
What Fun!

Step 3

Every child loves playtime, and little blue and little yellow are no exceptions! Have each student, in turn, show the class her playtime picture. Ask her to say and complete the following sentence starter to tell about it: "Little blue and little yellow…" After every student has shared her work, have her write a one-sentence caption below the line on her paper (or ask her to dictate a caption for an adult to write). Compile the completed illustrations into a class book titled "Playtime for Little Blue and Little Yellow." Lead a shared reading of the book, inviting each youngster to read her page aloud.

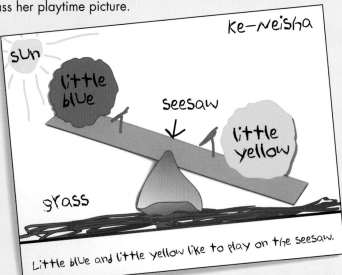

Playtime Picture

Follow the directions.

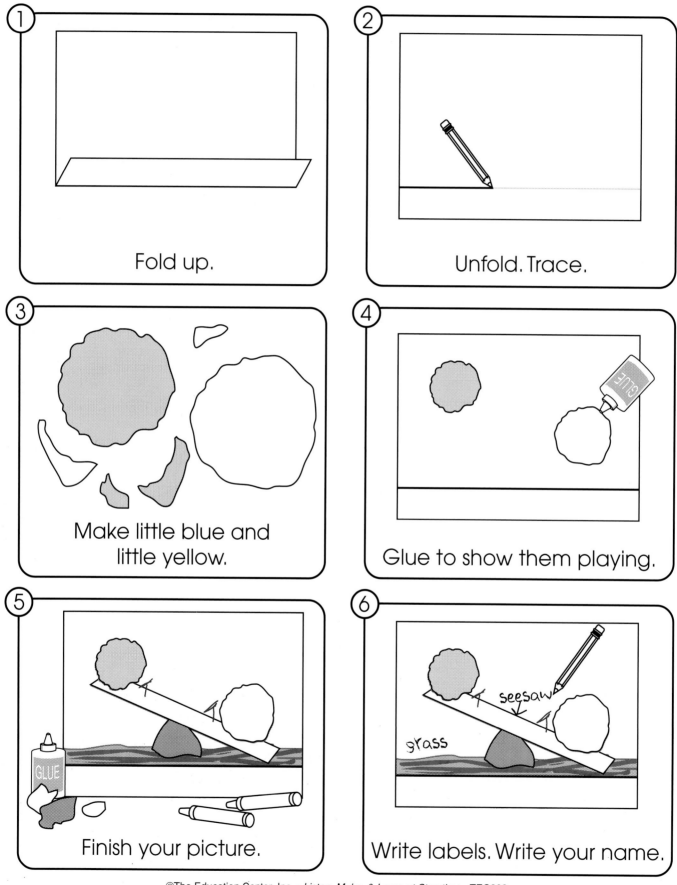

1. Fold up.

2. Unfold. Trace.

3. Make little blue and little yellow.

4. Glue to show them playing.

5. Finish your picture.

6. Write labels. Write your name.

seesaw

grass

GLUE

Note to the teacher: Use with the *Little Blue and Little Yellow* unit that begins on page 108.

Name

Today We Play

Here are some fun things to play with!
Write to label.
Color.

Note to the teacher: Use with the *Little Blue and Little Yellow* unit that begins on page 108.

Make Way for Ducklings

Written and illustrated by Robert McCloskey

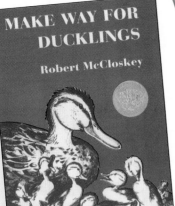

After searching Boston for the perfect place to raise their family, Mr. and Mrs. Mallard settle on the banks of the Charles River. Mrs. Mallard later walks her eight ducklings through the busy streets to visit the nearby Public Garden. The Caldecott Medal–winning illustrations of this beloved classic provide a delightful portrayal of the endearing duck family and the heartwarming effect it has on the city folks.

Skills: Read common word families. Blend onsets and rimes.

Teacher Preparation

Literature selection: Preview a copy of *Make Way for Ducklings.*

Craft:

- Cut several kitchen sponges into small pieces for students to share at a center. Clip a clothespin to each piece for easy handling.

- If desired, cover students' work area with newspaper for easy cleanup. Set out shallow containers of yellow tempera paint.

- For each child, make a white construction paper copy of page 115 and then use a craft knife to cut out the indicated window.

- Gather the remaining student materials listed below.

- For the literacy link activity on the following page, obtain five small sheets of chart paper. Also program five sets of blank cards with the following letters (one letter per card): *B, D, M, R, S, T, V, Z.*

Student Materials

Each student needs the following:
- copy of page 114
- prepared copy of page 115 (See instructions above.)
- access to yellow tempera paint and a precut sponge with a clothespin
- yellow craft feather
- 10 mm wiggle eye
- craft stick
- crayons
- scissors
- glue
- tape
- brad

Begin With a Book
Make Way for Ducklings

The Mallard family in this story belongs to an even larger family—the *-ack* word family! Show students the book cover. Tell students that the ducklings have names that belong to the same word family. Ask them to guess the names. Read the story aloud to check their guesses. Then have students recall the ducklings' actual names. List the names on a sheet of chart paper and ask volunteers to underline the *-ack* word ending in each one. Point to each name, in turn, as you lead students in reading the list. To explore more word family names, give each student the materials listed on page 112. Then use the provided directions to help him make a dapper duck puppet.

Continue With a Craft
Dapper Duck Puppet

Directions:
1. Direct each child to color his duck's bill and feet and the background of the pattern.
2. Instruct him to cut out the duck pattern and the word family wheel.
3. Have him carefully sponge-paint the duck's body.
4. When the paint is dry, ask him to glue a feather onto the duck's body to resemble a wing. Then have him glue on a wiggle eye.
5. Direct him to tape the craft stick to the back of the pattern to make a puppet.
6. Help him use the brad to attach the word family wheel to the puppet where indicated.

Link With a Literacy Skill
Ducky Word Family Fun

From Jack to Quack, all of the ducklings' names belong to the *-ack* word family! To make more ducky word family names, divide students into five groups. Give each group a set of consonant cards and a sheet of chart paper. Assign each group a different word family and have each group member turn his puppet wheel to reveal it in the window. Then have each group use its cards and the word family to create silly duck names. Ask the students to write the names on their paper.

After a designated work period, invite each group to present its list. To do so, each group member, in turn, holds his puppet and uses the following format to introduce himself: "I'm [name] from the [word family] duck family." The students repeat this process until they have read all of their listed names.

Dapper Duck Puppet

Follow the directions.

1. Color the duck's bill and feet. Color the background.

2. Cut.

3. Use a sponge to paint the duck. Let it dry.

4. Glue on a wing. Glue on an eye.

5. Tape.

6. Use a brad to connect the circles.

Note to the teacher: Use with the *Make Way for Ducklings* unit that begins on page 112.

Use with the *Make Way for Ducklings* unit that begins on page 112.

-ack

-op

-an

-est

-ip

-at

Mama Cat Has Three Kittens

Written and illustrated by Denise Fleming

Bold handmade-paper illustrations and predictable text capture the antics of two kittens, Fluffy and Skinny, as they imitate Mama Cat. Their brother, Boris, however, is shown lazing in the sun. When he finally decides to join in the fun, it's too late because the rest of the family is napping. What's a kitten to do? Why, take another nap of course!

Skills: Explore story vocabulary.
Dramatize a story.

Teacher Preparation

Literature selection: Preview a copy of *Mama Cat Has Three Kittens*.

Craft:

- Set out shallow containers of tempera paint in assorted catlike colors, such as orange, brown, and yellow. Cut several sponges into small pieces for students to share. Clip a clothespin onto each piece for easy handling. Place at least one prepared sponge by each container of paint.

- Cover students' work area with newspaper for easy cleanup, if desired.

- Gather the remaining student materials listed below.

Extension: If desired, make a copy of page 119 for each student to complete at the conclusion of the literacy link activity described on page 117.

Student Materials

Each student needs the following:
- copy of page 118
- 9" paper plate
- assorted colors of tempera paint and prepared sponges (See instructions above.)
- assorted construction paper scraps
- 3 white pipe cleaners
- jumbo craft stick
- black marker
- pencil
- scissors
- glue
- tape

Begin With a Book

Mama Cat Has Three Kittens

Oh, the life of a cat! Invite students to brainstorm things that cats do. List the corresponding verbs on the chalkboard. Tell students that the characters in the featured book are a mama cat and three kittens. Also reveal that some of the characters have a very busy day. As you read the story aloud, ask students to think about how the brainstormed list of verbs compares with the cats' actions. Then invite them to share their observations. Add any newly identified cat-related verbs to the list. To bring the cats' antics to life, distribute the materials listed on page 116. Have each student refer to the illustrated directions as you use the steps below to guide her in making a "purr-fect" kitten mask!

Continue With a Craft

Kitty Craft

Directions:

1. Have each student write her name on the front of her plate and then turn the plate over.
2. Instruct her to sponge-paint the back of the plate to resemble cat fur. Let the paint dry.
3. Direct her to fashion two cat ears and a nose from the construction paper. Then have her glue them in place.
4. Tell her to use a marker to draw two eyes and a mouth.
5. Use the tip of a pencil to poke a hole through the plate on each side of the nose. Then help the child thread the pipe cleaners through the holes to make whiskers as shown below.
6. Have her tape the craft stick to the back of the plate to make a handle.

Link With a Literacy Skill

"Meow-velous" Movements

Mama Cat, Fluffy, and Skinny have so much fun that even lazy Boris wants to join them! Invite your students to get in on the action with this dramatization. To begin, ask students to pantomime selected actions from the story. If desired, also have them pantomime other actions brainstormed earlier. Next, assign each character's role to a different student. As you slowly reread the story, have each student actor hold her mask and perform the appropriate actions. Encourage the remaining students to chime in each time you read "Boris naps." Then lead the class in a round of applause for the young actors. Ask the actors to return to their places; then reassign the roles. Repeat the process until every student has had a turn to perform.

Step 1

Step 2

Step 3

117

Kitty Craft

Follow the directions.

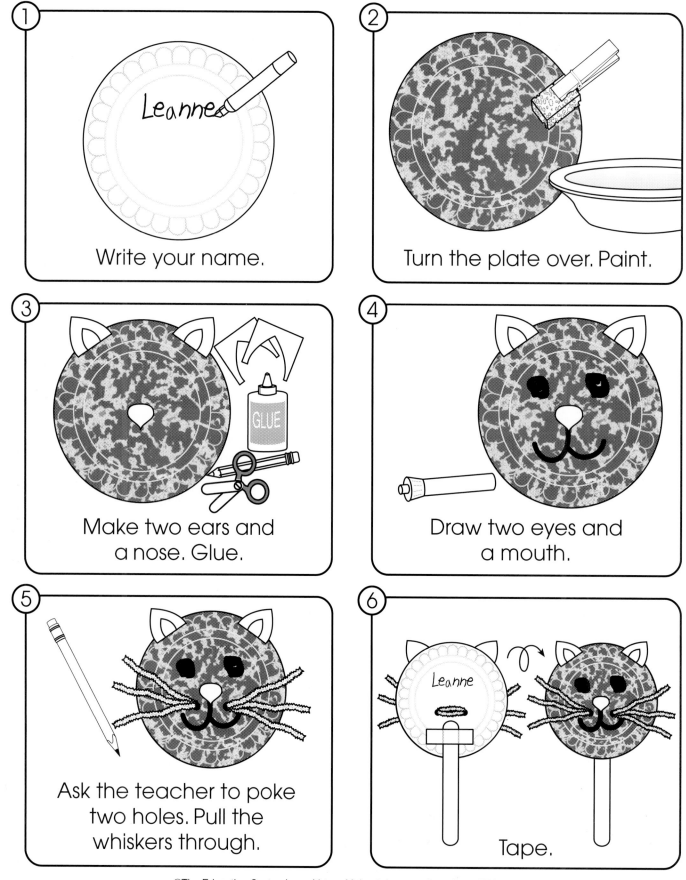

1. Write your name.

2. Turn the plate over. Paint.

3. Make two ears and a nose. Glue.

4. Draw two eyes and a mouth.

5. Ask the teacher to poke two holes. Pull the whiskers through.

6. Tape.

©The Education Center, Inc. • *Listen, Make, & Learn at Storytime* • TEC893

Note to the teacher: Use with the *Mama Cat Has Three Kittens* unit that begins on page 116.

Name _____

Oh, Boris!

Read each sentence.
Connect the dots to show the missing word.
Color.

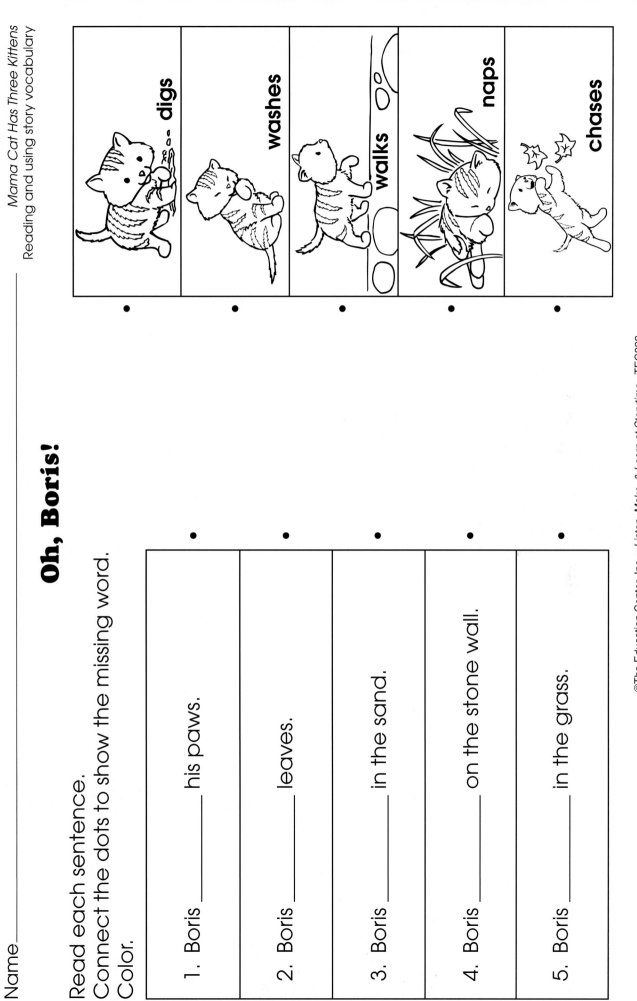

digs

washes

walks

naps

chases

1. Boris _____ his paws.

2. Boris _____ leaves.

3. Boris _____ in the sand.

4. Boris _____ on the stone wall.

5. Boris _____ in the grass.

Note to the teacher: Use with the *Mama Cat Has Three Kittens* unit that begins on page 116.

Marianthe's Story: Painted Words Spoken Memories

Written and illustrated by Aliki

This unique two-sided book tells the story of Mari, a young girl from a faraway country. Unable to speak, read, or write English, Mari uses her artwork to communicate with her new classmates. Finally, after time spent listening, learning, and being gently encouraged by her insightful teacher, she is ready to tell the class her life story.

Skill: Tell about a memorable event in correct sequence.

Teacher Preparation

Literature selection: Preview a copy of *Marianthe's Story.*

Craft:
- Cover students' work area with newspaper for easy cleanup, if desired.
- Set out watercolor paints, water, and paintbrushes.
- Gather the remaining student materials listed below.

Student Materials

Each student needs the following:
- copy of page 122
- construction paper copy of page 123
- 6" x 8" piece of white construction paper
- access to watercolor paint, water, and a paintbrush
- two 36" lengths of yarn
- glue
- scissors
- tape

Begin With a Book
Marianthe's Story

A new country. A new school. A new language. No wonder Mari is afraid! To help students make personal connections with Mari's situation, ask them to recall times when they were nervous or frightened. Invite volunteers to describe how they felt and why. Explain that Mari, the book's main character, is scared at the beginning of the story, but is more content at its conclusion. Ask students to listen carefully as you read the book aloud to find out why Mari is frightened and how she conquers her fear. Then have students share their observations. Guide students to realize that as Mari and her classmates become better acquainted, Mari feels more comfortable. To help your students use their artwork to learn more about each other, give each youngster the materials listed on page 120. Use the provided directions to help him convey a story about a memorable event in his own life.

Continue With a Craft
Fancy Frame

Directions:
1. Instruct each student to paint on the white paper a picture of a memorable event he would like to share with the class. Allow the paint to dry.
2. Have him cut along the inner and outer bold lines of the frame.
3. Direct him to trace the inner dotted line with glue. Have him carefully place a length of yarn along the glue and then gently pat it in place.
4. Ask him to repeat the process with the second dotted line. Let the glue dry.
5. Have him trim the excess yarn.
6. Instruct him to tape the painting to the back of the frame so that the picture shows through the opening.

Link With a Literacy Skill
Stories to Tell

Mr. Petrie knows that artwork can be a powerful communication tool. It can be even more powerful when combined with storytelling! Remind students that Mari started at the beginning of her life story and told the events in order. Point out that if she had told the events out of sequence, it would have been difficult to understand. Next, invite a student to show his artwork to the class. Ask him to tell about the event it represents in sequence. (Prompt him with transition words such as *first, then,* and *next,* as appropriate.) Lead the class in a round of applause for the young storyteller; then invite a different student to tell his story. Repeat the process with a desired number of students each day until every youngster has been in the spotlight.

Fancy Frame

Follow the directions.

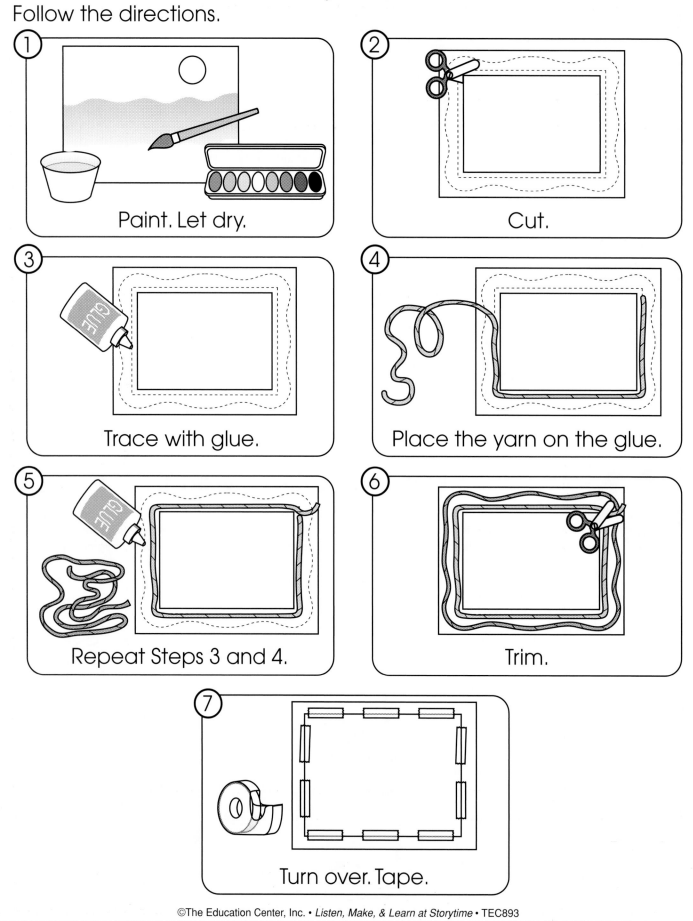

1. Paint. Let dry.

2. Cut.

3. Trace with glue.

4. Place the yarn on the glue.

5. Repeat Steps 3 and 4.

6. Trim.

7. Turn over. Tape.

Note to the teacher: Use with the *Marianthe's Story* unit that begins on page 120.

Miss Bindergarten Gets Ready for Kindergarten

Written by Joseph Slate
Illustrated by Ashley Wolff

With excitement, rhyme, and plenty of colorful illustrations, Miss Bindergarten and her 26 students busily prepare for the much anticipated first day of kindergarten. Youngsters will enjoy seeing how the animal students get ready in alphabetical order. But the big thrill is watching Miss B. set up her classroom in record time!

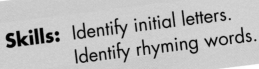

Skills: Identify initial letters.
Identify rhyming words.

Teacher Preparation

Literature selection: Preview a copy of *Miss Bindergarten Gets Ready for Kindergarten*.

Craft:
• Cut a 28-inch length of yarn for each child. Knot each end.

• Gather the remaining student materials listed below.

Extension: If desired, make a copy of page 127 for each student to complete at the conclusion of the literacy link activity described on page 125.

Student Materials

Each student needs the following:
• copy of page 126
• 6" square of black construction paper
• prepared yarn length (See instructions above.)
• access to Crayola Construction Paper crayons
• 4 jumbo craft sticks
• fine-tipped black marker
• white crayon
• stapler
• glue

Begin With a Book

Miss Bindergarten Gets Ready for Kindergarten

What did you do to get ready for the first day of school? Share some highlights with your students, then prompt them to tell about their own preparations. As you read the featured book aloud, encourage students to listen carefully to find out how Miss B. and her class prepared for the first day. Prompt a class discussion about the similarities between the characters' preparations and those you and your students made. Next, distribute the materials listed on page 124. Ask each youngster to refer to the illustrated steps as you use the directions below to help her create a nametag necklace for the first day of school.

Step 1

Continue With a Craft

Nifty Nametag Necklace

Directions:
1. Help each student staple the yarn ends to adjacent corners of her paper to create a hanger. Have her turn the paper over and position it so that the hanger is at the top.
2. Ask her to use a colored Crayola Construction Paper crayon to write the first letter of her name. Then have her use a white crayon to finish writing it.
3. Direct her to use a black marker to draw lines on the craft sticks as shown below.
4. To make a frame, have her glue a craft stick to both sides of the paper. Then instruct her to glue a craft stick to the top and bottom of the paper.

Step 2

Link With a Literacy Skill

The Name of the Game

What's in a name? Plenty of practice with letters, sounds, and rhymes! Revisit the featured book with students. Then reread the book, pausing at desired intervals to point out the highlighted letter in each student's name and the accompanying rhyming text. Next, invite each child to don the nametag that she made. Have every student walk along an established route around the classroom and introduce herself to her classmates. Encourage each youngster to listen carefully to the names and study her classmates' nametags to determine whether another student's name begins with the same letter as hers. Then gather students in a circle. Have each child, in turn, say the first letter of her name and then her whole name. Help students identify names that start with the same letter and any name pairs that rhyme. What a letter-perfect way to start the school year!

Step 3

Nifty Nametag Necklace

Follow the directions.

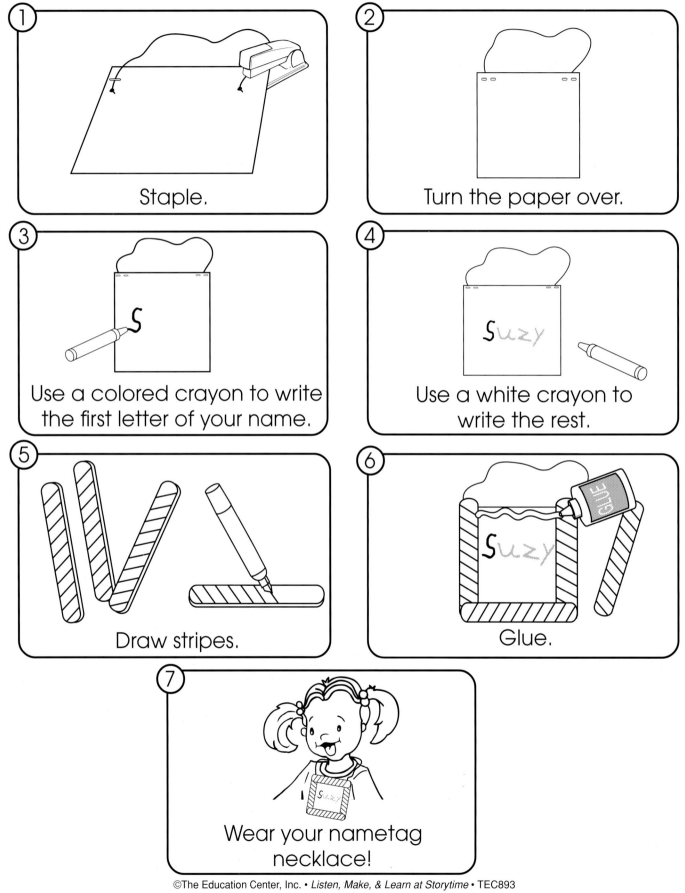

1. Staple.

2. Turn the paper over.

3. Use a colored crayon to write the first letter of your name.

4. Use a white crayon to write the rest.

5. Draw stripes.

6. Glue.

7. Wear your nametag necklace!

Note to the teacher: Use with the *Miss Bindergarten Gets Ready for Kindergarten* unit that begins on page 124.

Name _____

Color.
Read the words.
Cut and glue to show the rhymes.

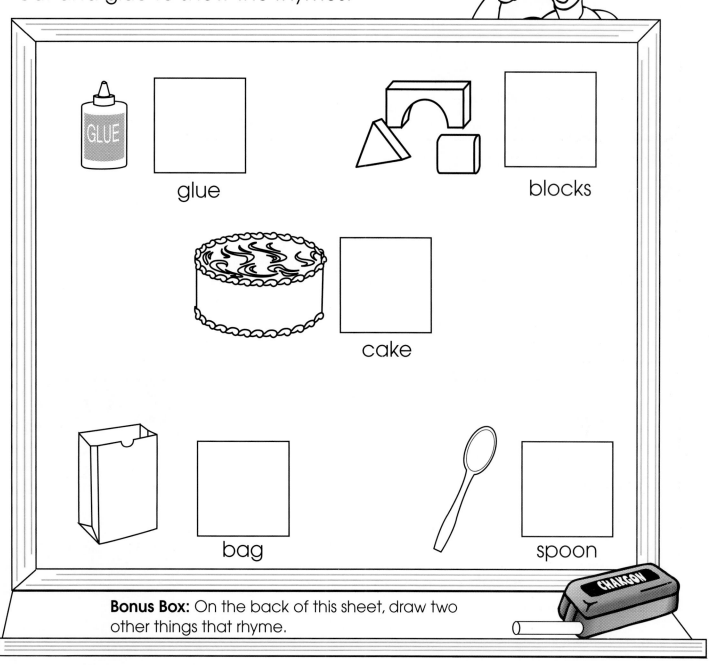

glue

blocks

cake

bag

spoon

Bonus Box: On the back of this sheet, draw two other things that rhyme.

socks   flag   shoe   snake   moon

Note to the teacher: Use with the *Miss Bindergarten Gets Ready for Kindergarten* unit that begins on page 124.

Miss Spider's Tea Party

Written and illustrated by David Kirk

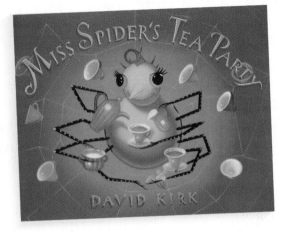

Miss Spider longs to have friends! But insects steer clear of the lonely arachnid since spiders have a reputation for harming bugs. All that changes, though, the day a fragile, wet moth enjoys a tasty snack with Miss Spider. The vibrant oil-painted illustrations seem almost three-dimensional, making this book a captivating read-aloud selection.

Skill: Describe a character.

Teacher Preparation

Literature selection: Preview a copy of *Miss Spider's Tea Party*.

Craft:

• Gather the student materials listed below.

Extension: If desired, make a copy of page 131 for each student to complete at the conclusion of the literacy link activity described on page 129.

Student Materials

Each student needs the following:
• copy of page 130
• 3" yellow tagboard or poster board circle
• 6" yellow tagboard or poster board circle
• eight 6" black pipe cleaner lengths
• length of string
• access to a hole puncher
• crayons or markers
• glue

Begin With a Book

Miss Spider's Tea Party

Count on students to go buggy over this rhyming tale of friendship! Show students the book cover and read the title aloud. Ask students whether spiders really drink tea. After confirming that spiders are not tea drinkers, explain that real spiders eat insects. Read the book aloud. Then guide students to contrast the insects' initial perceptions of Miss Spider with their perceptions of her at the end of the book. Next, distribute the materials listed on page 128. Have each child refer to his illustrated directions as you use the steps below to help him make a Miss Spider look-alike.

Continue With a Craft

Spider Friend

1. Ask each child to illustrate Miss Spider's face on the small circle. Have him glue the small and large circles together to resemble a spider head and body.
2. Have him flip the spider and color the large circle to resemble Miss Spider's back.
3. Instruct him to hole-punch four holes on each side of the large circle. Provide assistance as necessary.
4. Direct him to insert one end of each pipe cleaner length in a different hole and then bend the pipe cleaner to secure it. Ask him to shape the pipe cleaners to resemble spider legs.
5. Instruct him to hole-punch the top of his project. Have him thread a string through the hole and then knot the ends to make a hanger.

Link With a Literacy Skill

Spidery Words

Miss Spider's quest for visitors reveals a lot about her personality! Ask students why they think the bugs don't want to be near Miss Spider at first. Lead them to conclude that the bugs are afraid of her. Point out that once the bugs become better acquainted with Miss Spider, they know they have nothing to fear and they become friends with her.

To enhance students' understanding of Miss Spider, ask them to listen carefully for more information about her during a second reading. Then invite students to brainstorm a list of words that tell about the character, encouraging them to support their suggestions with story details. Next, ask each youngster to write on the front of his project three words that he thinks best describe the unique arachnid. Suspend students' spiders from the ceiling to create an eye-catching reminder that friends come in many unexpected sizes, shapes, and colors.

lonely
sad
friendly

Spider Friend

Follow the directions.

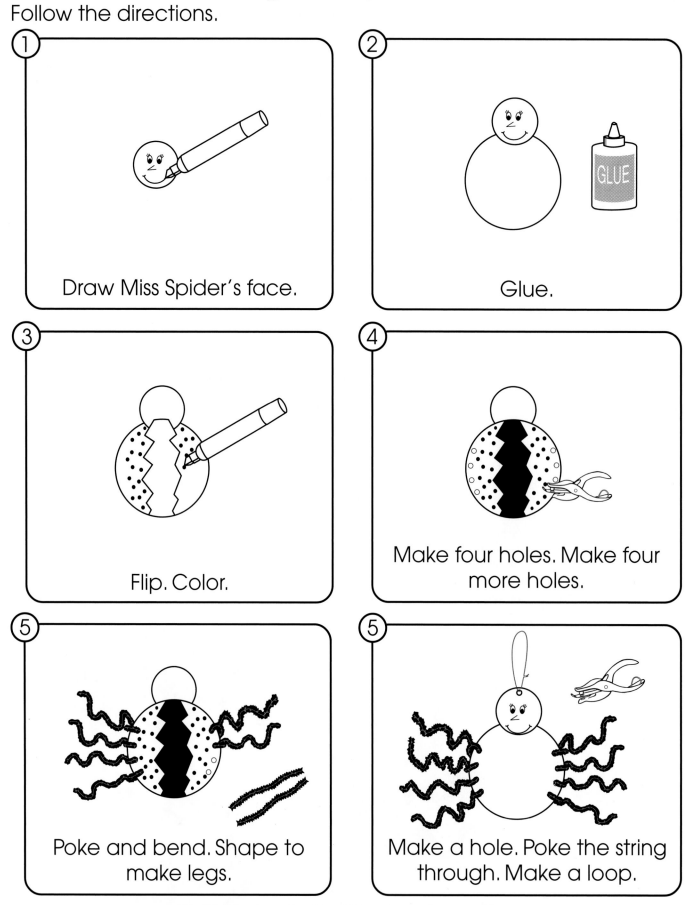

① Draw Miss Spider's face.

② Glue.

③ Flip. Color.

④ Make four holes. Make four more holes.

⑤ Poke and bend. Shape to make legs.

⑤ Make a hole. Poke the string through. Make a loop.

Note to the teacher: Use with the *Miss Spider's Tea Party* unit that begins on page 128.

Name _____

Tea Time!

Make a path to the tea party!
Begin at the star.
Color each word that tells about Miss Spider.

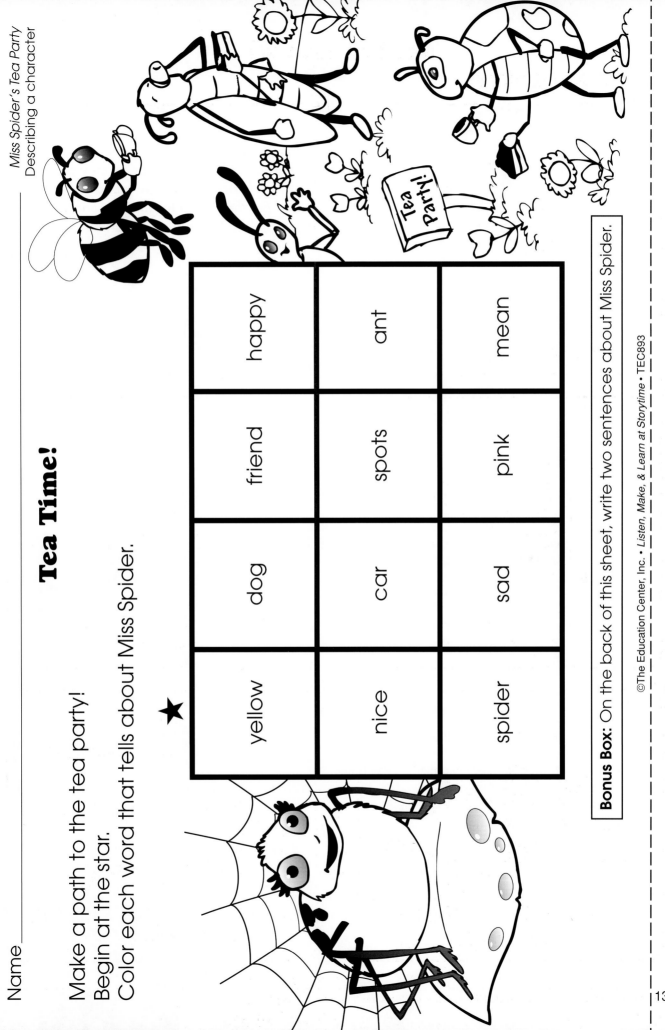

★

yellow	dog	friend	happy
nice	car	spots	ant
spider	sad	pink	mean

Bonus Box: On the back of this sheet, write two sentences about Miss Spider.

Note to the teacher: Use with the *Miss Spider's Tea Party* unit that begins on page 128.

131

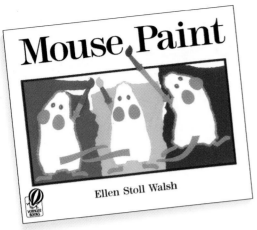

Ellen Stoll Walsh

Mouse Paint
Written and illustrated by Ellen Stoll Walsh

In this award-winning selection, three curious white mice make intriguing and colorful discoveries as they play in paint. The mice eagerly apply their newfound knowledge to a painting project. But they don't forget how important white is to them—especially when a cat is nearby!

Skills: Share observations orally or in writing. Recall details.

Teacher Preparation

Literature selection: Preview a copy of *Mouse Paint*.

Craft:

- Make a white construction paper copy of page 135 for each student. Use a craft knife to cut out the indicated ear openings.

- Gather the remaining student materials listed below.

- For the literacy link activity described on the following page, obtain paintbrushes, white paper, writing paper, and yellow, red, and blue paint.

Student Materials

Each student needs the following:
- copy of page 134
- prepared white construction paper copy of page 135 (See instructions above.)
- 2½" square of orange, purple, and green construction paper
- 2 brads
- popsicle stick
- crayons
- scissors
- glue

Begin With a Book
Mouse Paint

A bit of mischief leads to a colorful sequence of events in this mouse tale! Ask students to imagine what would happen if mice played with paint. Invite youngsters to share their ideas; then read the book aloud. Point out that the characters learn a lot as they play because they are observant. Revisit selected pages and ask volunteers to share their observations about the illustrations. Prompt them to include details about mixing colors and seeing the mice against backgrounds of various colors. Next, give each student the materials listed on page 132. Have her use the illustrated steps as you refer to the directions below to help her make a color-savvy mouse.

Step 1

Continue With a Craft
Playful Mouse

Directions:

1. Instruct each child to color the mouse's ears and paws brown. Have her color the paintbrush tip as desired. Direct her to color the sections of each wheel yellow, blue, and red.
2. Ask her to cut out the patterns.
3. Help her use brads to fasten the wheels behind the ears.
4. Have her glue each paw to the mouse pattern as indicated.
5. Instruct her to glue the paintbrush tip to the popsicle stick. Ask her to glue the popsicle stick to the underside of one paw.
6. Direct her to trace the line indicated on the jar with glue. Have her fold up the jar on the line.
7. Ask her to place the construction paper squares in the flap as shown below.

Step 2

Link With a Literacy Skill
Colorful Combinations

Students' completed projects are a perfect tool for reviewing the characters' colorful discoveries! Ask each youngster to remove the paper squares from the holder of her mouse project. Begin re-reading the book to students, pausing on the page that shows the red mouse dancing in the yellow paint. Have each student turn the wheels on her project to show red and yellow. Then ask her to silently recall the color that results when these two colors are mixed. Instruct her to place the corresponding square in the holder and then hold up her project. Scan the projects for accuracy and then continue reading to reveal the actual result. Review how the mice created green and purple in a like manner.

For added learning fun, have students use the provided painting supplies to re-create the characters' color-mixing experiments. Then have each youngster summarize her observations on a sheet of writing paper.

Step 3

Playful Mouse

Follow the directions.

1. Color the ears and paws. Color the top of the paintbrush.

2. Color the wheels yellow, blue, and red.

3. Cut.

4. Attach the wheels.

5. Trace with glue. Place the paws.

6. Glue to the stick. Glue to the paw.

7. Trace with glue. Fold up.

8. Put the squares in the flap.

Note to the teacher: Use with the *Mouse Paint* unit that begins on page 132.

Use with the *Mouse Paint* unit that begins on page 132.

Glue.

Glue.

Glue.

Mr. Griggs' Work

Written by Cynthia Rylant
Illustrated by Julie Downing

Mr. Griggs is so passionate about his work at the post office that he thinks about it constantly. Whether he's taking a bath, washing dishes, or enjoying a walk, the loyal postal worker is always reflecting on the details of his job. Pastel illustrations tenderly capture Mr. Griggs's fondness for his work and his disappointment when he needs to stay home one day.

Skills: Read common word families.
Sort words by word families.

Teacher Preparation

Literature selection: Preview a copy of *Mr. Griggs' Work*. Write the letter shown on a sheet of chart paper.

> Dear [teacher's name],
>   Is there something you love to do so much that you think about it day and night? There is for me. <u>Mr. Griggs' Work</u> tells all about it. Please read this book to your students so they can learn about the best job ever!
>
>   Your friend,
>   Mr. Griggs

Craft:

• Gather the student materials listed below.

• Make a copy of page 139 for each student to use with the literacy link activity on the following page.

Student Materials

Each student needs the following:
• copy of page 138
• 9" x 12" sheet of blue construction paper
• access to a stapler
• crayon or fine-tipped marker
• scissors

Begin With a Book

Mr. Griggs' Work

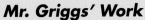

Deliver a touching example of tireless dedication with this first-class story! Display the prepared letter and read it aloud with students. Verbally respond to the question in the letter and invite volunteers to do the same. Ask students to share their ideas about the plot of the mentioned book and the identity of the letter's author. Then read the book aloud to check their ideas. At the book's conclusion, have students recall Mr. Griggs' mail-related responsibilities. Tell youngsters that they will each imitate an important part of his job—sorting the mail. To prepare for this task, give each student the materials listed on page 136. Have him refer to the illustrated directions as you use the steps below to guide him in creating a mini mailbox.

Continue With a Craft

Mini Mailbox

Directions:
1. Have each student fold his paper in half to 6" x 9".
2. Tell him to position the paper vertically and round the top two corners.
3. Instruct him to cut two parallel slits at the bottom of the paper (each about 1½ inches from a side). Have him fold up the resulting flap.
4. Direct him to turn the mailbox over. Have him staple the flap in place. Then instruct him to staple the side opposite the fold, leaving the top open.
5. Have him use a marker or crayon to draw details on the mailbox as illustrated. Then direct him to personalize it.

Link With a Literacy Skill

Sort It Out!

Mr. Griggs takes care to deliver every envelope to the intended recipient. Have your students follow suit and "deliver" envelopes to the correct families—word families, that is. Pair students and give each youngster a copy of page 139. Instruct each student to cut out the houses and envelopes along the bold lines. Have him place the row of houses on a work surface and the envelopes in the mailbox that he made. Direct students in each twosome to alternate turns.

To take a turn, a youngster removes an envelope from his mailbox, reads it aloud, and then places it on the house labeled with the corresponding word family. The partners continue until all their mail has been delivered. When every twosome has finished sorting its mail, verify the words for each word family. Then have each youngster tuck his houses and envelopes in his mailbox for easy home delivery!

137

Mini Mailbox

Follow the directions.

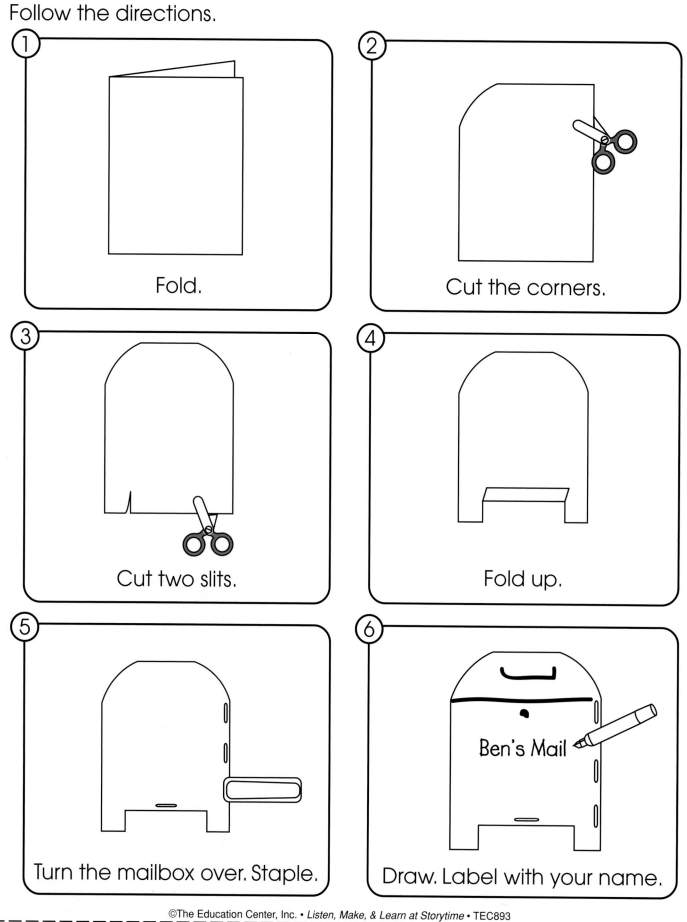

1. Fold.

2. Cut the corners.

3. Cut two slits.

4. Fold up.

5. Turn the mailbox over. Staple.

6. Draw. Label with your name.

Ben's Mail

©The Education Center, Inc. • *Listen, Make, & Learn at Storytime* • TEC893

Note to the teacher: Use with the *Mr. Griggs' Work* unit that begins on page 136.

Patterns

Use with the *Mr. Griggs' Work* unit that begins on page 136.

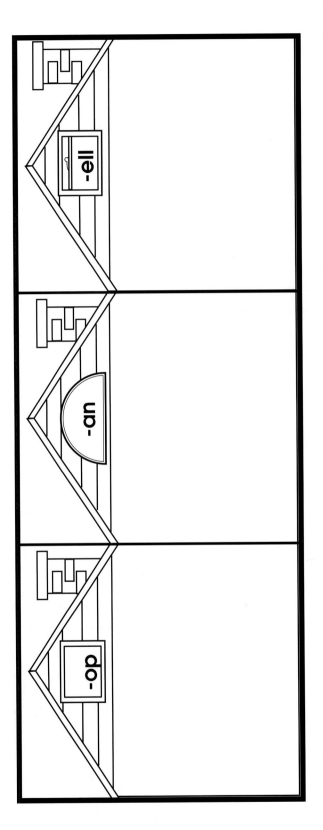

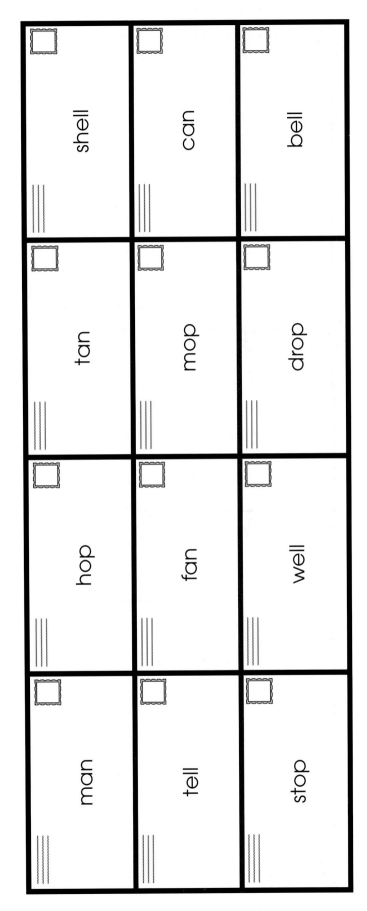

The Napping House

Written by Audrey Wood
Illustrated by Don Wood

From the snoring granny to the slumbering mouse, everyone in this award-winning book is grabbing some shut-eye. Everyone but a pesky little flea, that is! Luminescent illustrations capture the dreaminess of the night and the bright approach of the dawn, creating a spellbinding cumulative tale.

Skills: Explore story vocabulary.
Retell a story.

Teacher Preparation

Literature selection: Preview a copy of *The Napping House*.

Craft:
- For each student, mark the center of one long edge of a 9" x 12" sheet of construction paper.

- Gather the remaining student materials listed below.

Student Materials

Each student needs the following:
- copy of page 142
- white construction paper copy of page 143
- 9" x 12" sheet of marked construction paper
- resealable plastic sandwich bag
- small black pom-pom
- 12" length of yarn
- crayons
- scissors
- tape
- glue

Begin With a Book

The Napping House

This humorous tale introduces youngsters to a dreamy collection of vocabulary words! Write "napping" on the chalkboard. Confirm students' understanding of the word and then ask them to brainstorm other sleep-related words. List them on the chalkboard. Tell students that *The Napping House* is about several characters who are sleeping. As you share the book, encourage students to listen carefully to find out how the author describes each character.

At the book's conclusion, read the listed words aloud. Revisit the book as needed to help students recall other sleep-related words. Add the words to the list. Then give each student the materials listed on page 140. Have her refer to the illustrated steps as you help her make a cozy house for the sleepy characters (and wakeful flea!).

Step 1

Continue With a Craft

Cozy House

Directions:

1. Instruct each student to glue one end of the string to the pom-pom. Allow it to dry.
2. Ask her to place the blank sheet of construction paper horizontally on a work surface so that the mark is at the bottom. Instruct her to fold over each side to meet at the mark.
3. To make a roof, direct her to cut away the top corners. (See the illustration below.)
4. Ask her to use crayons to add details to the folded paper so that it resembles a house.
5. Have her color the patterns and then cut them out. Instruct her to store them in the plastic resealable bag.
6. Direct her to tape the free end of the string to the back of the house near the center of the bottom edge.

Step 2

Link With a Literacy Skill

A Story to Sleep On

Handy props and a cumulative story combine to make students right at home with retelling! Have each student place her folded house on a work surface. Instruct her to remove each pattern from her bag and position the string so that it extends beyond the roof. After telling students that the pom-pom represents the flea in the story, confirm that they can identify the patterns. As you slowly reread the book to the class, ask each youngster to act out the story with her props. Provide time for each student to retell the story to a classmate. Then encourage her to take the props home to use in a retelling for her family. Sweet dreams of retelling success are guaranteed!

Step 3

141

Cozy House

Follow the directions.

1 Glue. Let dry.

2 Place with the mark at the bottom. Fold to the mark.

3 Fold to the mark.

4 Cut to make a roof.

5 Color to finish the house.

6 Color. Cut out. Put the patterns in the bag.

7 Tape.

Note to the teacher: Use with *The Napping House* unit that begins on page 140.

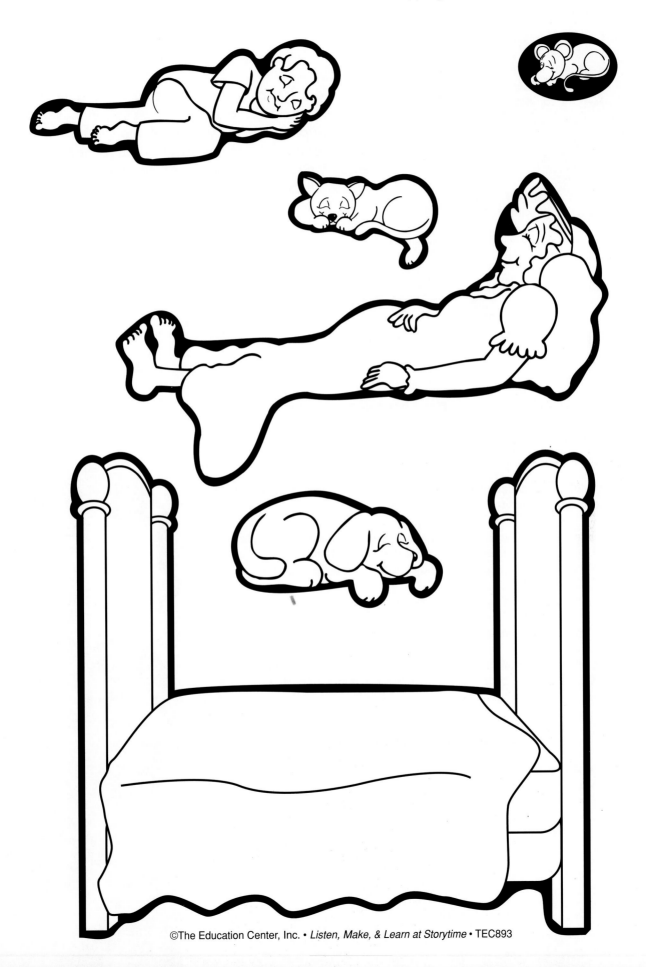

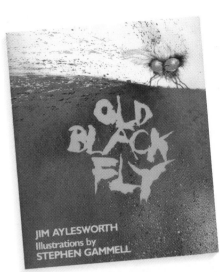

Old Black Fly

Written by Jim Aylesworth
Illustrated by Stephen Gammell

Old black fly has quite an adventure one summer day! He annoys an entire household by getting into everything from the apple pie to the yarn in Mama's lap—until the baby takes matters into her own hands. Youngsters are sure to enjoy the rollicking rhythm and lively illustrations in this unique alphabet book.

Skill: Apply letter-sound correspondences.

Teacher Preparation

Literature selection: Preview a copy of *Old Black Fly*.

Craft:

- Obtain several clean toothbrushes and an equal number of craft sticks for splatter painting.

- Cover students' work area with newspaper. Set out shallow containers of thinned, washable tempera paint in several different colors. Place a toothbrush in each container and a craft stick beside each one.

- If desired, provide a paint shirt for each child.

- Gather the remaining student materials listed below.

- For the literacy link activity on page 145, make a copy of page 147 for each child. Provide access to crayons, scissors, and glue.

Student Materials

Each student needs the following:
- copy of page 146
- access to prepared paint, toothbrushes, and craft sticks (See instructions above.)
- 12" x 18" sheet of white construction paper

Begin With a Book

Old Black Fly

Mischievous old black fly gets into anything and everything! Ask students if flies have ever bothered them. Then tell students that the family in this book gets very annoyed by a pesky little fly. Read the story aloud, pausing after a few pages to ask students what they notice about the fly's path. Guide students to notice that his path is in alphabetical order. Continue reading, inviting youngsters to predict the next letter before turning each page.

At the book's conclusion, revisit several pages with students and ask them to study the illustrations. Tell students that each of them will make an illustration that has a similar style. Distribute the materials listed on page 144 and use the directions below to help students make splatter paintings.

Continue With a Craft

Pesky Fly Painting

Directions:
1. If desired, invite each child in a small group to don a paint shirt before joining you at the paint center.
2. Demonstrate how to dip a toothbrush in paint, hold the bristles over a sheet of paper, and then splatter the paint by slowly drawing a craft stick across the bristles and toward your body.
3. Encourage each child to splatter-paint on his paper in a like manner, using different colors and continuing until he is satisfied with the result.
4. Allow the paint to dry.

Link With a Literacy Skill

Alphabet Trip

Old black fly went buzzin' through the alphabet and your youngsters can too! Assign a different letter to each student. (If you have a large class, assign the same letter to more than one student.) Give each student a copy of page 147. Ask him to write his assigned letter in the provided box on the frame. Have him illustrate an object that begins with the letter and then color the frame. Help him write the corresponding word in the blank. Ask him to cut out the frame and box.

Next, return each painting to its owner. Have each youngster glue his frame and box to the painting as shown below. Alphabetically sequence the resulting pages and then bind them into a book titled "Buzzing Through the Alphabet." Gather students into a circle. As you display each page, in turn, lead the class in chanting the refrain up to the last word. Then have the child who illustrated the page chime in with the name of his chosen object.

Step 1

Step 2

Step 3

I have just been buzzin' around, buzzin' around, buzzin' around. I have just been buzzin' around, And this is what I saw: apple

145

Pesky Fly Painting

Follow the directions.

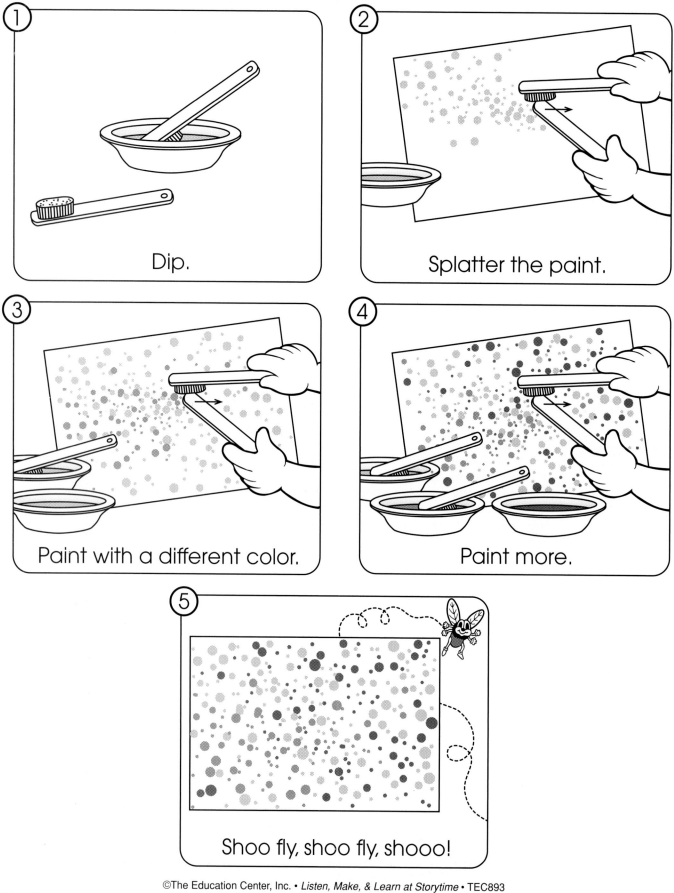

1. Dip.

2. Splatter the paint.

3. Paint with a different color.

4. Paint more.

5. Shoo fly, shoo fly, shooo!

Note to the teacher: Use with the *Old Black Fly* unit that begins on page 144.

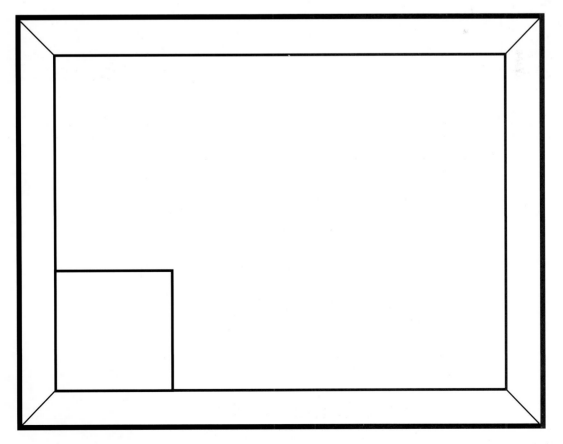

I have just been

buzzin' around,

buzzin' around,

buzzin' around.

I have just been

buzzin' around,

And this is what I saw:

_____

One Duck Stuck

Written by Phyllis Root
Illustrated by Jane Chapman

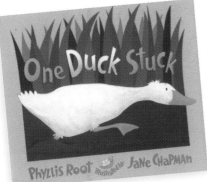

Splish! Clomp! Pleep! A variety of animals come to one duck's rescue down by the deep green marsh! Repetitive text and onomatopoeia bring the story to life as each critter, in turn, tries to help the duck stuck in the muck. Finally, the critters join forces and successfully free their muddy friend.

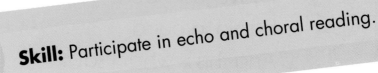

Skill: Participate in echo and choral reading.

Teacher Preparation

Literature selection: Preview a copy of *One Duck Stuck*.

Craft:

• Cut enough 9" x 12" sheets of white construction paper into quarters so that there are two quarters per student.

• Gather the student materials listed below.

Student Materials

Each student needs the following:

• copy of pages 150 and 151
• small white paper lunch bag
• 2 pieces of white construction paper (See instructions above.)
• orange crayon
• scissors
• glue

Step 1

Begin With a Book
One Duck Stuck

Oh, no! A duck is stuck in the muck! Show students the book cover and direct their attention to the duck's predicament. Invite them to offer their ideas for getting the duck unstuck. As you read the book aloud, encourage students to listen carefully to learn how the duck's problem is solved. At the end of the story, prompt a class discussion about what the animals learned in the process of helping the duck. *(Sometimes teamwork accomplishes more than individual efforts.)*

Next, tell students that the author incorporated patterns into the story. Guide students to notice details such as the refrain and the steadily increasing number of animals. Then distribute the materials listed on page 148. Refer to the provided directions to help students make a fine-feathered duck to use for more story-related fun!

Step 2

Continue With a Craft
Fine-Feathered Friend

Directions:
1. Have each student color the patterns on her copy of page 151 as shown. Then ask her to cut them out.
2. Instruct her to position the paper bag so that the flap is at the top. Ask her to glue the lower bill of the duck under the fold of the paper bag.
3. Direct her to glue the head to the flap.
4. Have her glue the feet onto the bottom of the bag as shown below.
5. Ask her to make a hand tracing on each piece of white paper. Have her cut out the tracings to make wings.
6. Instruct her to open the bag and then glue a wing to each side.

Step 3

Link With a Literacy Skill
Join the Chorus!

One Duck Stuck begs to be told by a chorus of voices, so what better way to have students put their fine-feathered puppets to use? Gather your students in a circle with their puppets. Hold the book open to the first page so that it is easily visible to every student. Read aloud "Down by the marsh," and ask students to echo the phrase. Read the remainder of the page, dividing it into easily repeated phrases and having students echo each one. To share the next page, direct students to use their puppets to take the duck's role and exclaim in unison "Help! Help! Who can help?" Continue with the story as described for the rest of the book. Then encourage each student to take her puppet home and use it to retell the ducky tale to her family.

Fine-Feathered Friend

Follow the directions.

1. Color.

2. Cut.

3. Glue the bill.

4. Glue the head.

5. Glue the feet.

6. Trace your hands.

7. Cut.

8. Open the bag. Glue the wings.

Note to the teacher: Use with the *One Duck Stuck* unit that begins on page 148.

Owl Moon

Written by Jane Yolen
Illustrated by John Schoenherr

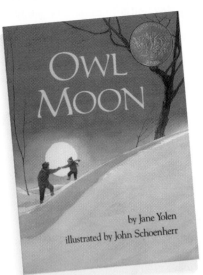

A young girl and her father wordlessly set out one cold winter night in search of owls. The girl has long awaited this night—her first time owling—and her patience does not go unrewarded. Award-winning watercolor illustrations beautifully capture the solitude of the majestic woods and the captivating appearance of the great owl.

Skill: Use descriptive words.

Teacher Preparation

Literature selection: Preview a copy of *Owl Moon*. Use sticky notes to mark two or three pages that have particularly good examples of descriptive words. Collect a real or artificial evergreen sprig and pinecone.

Craft:
- Cover students' work area with newspaper for easy cleanup, if desired.
- Set out shallow containers of green, brown, and blue tempera paint.
- Collect several real or artificial sprigs from evergreen boughs and pinecones. Set them near the paint.
- Gather the remaining student materials listed below.
- For the literacy link on the following page, each student will need one 9" x 12" sheet of green construction paper, one 4" x 6" piece of black construction paper, a blank 3" x 5" index card, and glue.

Extension: If desired, make a copy of page 155 for each student to complete at the conclusion of the literacy link activity described on page 153.

Student Materials

Each student needs the following:
- copy of page 154
- 9" x 12" sheet of white construction paper
- access to a real or artificial pinecone and evergreen sprig
- green, brown, and blue tempera paint
- cotton swab

Begin With a Book

Owl Moon

Take students on a memorable wintertime walk with this enchanting book! Show students an evergreen sprig and a pinecone. Explain that evergreens keep their leaves during the winter, unlike other trees, and that they bear pinecones. Tell students that the featured book takes place in the woods during winter. Read the book aloud; then encourage students to share details they noticed about the setting.

Next, prompt a class discussion that explores the girl's feelings about the owling adventure. Invite volunteers to recall wintertime experiences that were as memorable for them as this adventure is for the girl. Explain that each student will later write about such an experience. To make a booklet cover for his writing, give each youngster the materials listed on page 152. Have him refer to the illustrated steps as you use the directions below to help him create a woodsy painting.

Continue With a Craft

"Tree-mendous" Painting

Directions:
1. Have each youngster dip an evergreen sprig in green paint and then press it repeatedly onto his paper to make prints. Ask him to repeat the process until he is satisfied with the results.
2. Direct him to carefully dip a pinecone in brown paint and use it to make prints on the paper. Have him repeat the process as desired.
3. Instruct him to use the cotton swab and blue paint to make prints that resemble berries. Allow the paint to dry.

Link With a Literacy Skill

Picture This!

Encourage students to follow Yolen's example and use words to "paint" pictures! Tell students that the author of *Owl Moon* used well-chosen describing words to help readers and listeners picture the owling adventure. Ask students to listen carefully for describing words as you share the pages marked in the book. Then invite volunteers to recall the words.

Next, give each youngster a sheet of writing paper. Have him use describing words to write about a memorable wintertime experience. Ask him to staple his writing and a green sheet of construction paper behind his painting to make a booklet. Instruct him to write a title on a blank index card, glue the card onto the provided black paper, then glue the paper onto the cover. Invite each youngster to read his wintry writing to the class before taking it home to share with his family.

My Giant Snow Fort
by Jason

"Tree-mendous" Painting

Follow the directions.

1. Dip in green paint. Make prints.

2. Dip again. Make more prints.

3. Dip in brown paint. Make prints.

4. Dip again. Make more prints.

5. Dip in blue paint. Make dots. Let dry.

Note to the teacher: Use with the *Owl Moon* unit that begins on page 152.

In a Word

Read the word bank.
Choose the best word for each picture.
Write the word.

1.	2.	3.	4.	5.
	Who-o, who-o-o, who-o-o-o			
___	___	___	___	___

Word Bank

happy little
round tall
noisy

Choose two pictures.
Draw an X beside each one.
Use the words you wrote to tell about the pictures below.

A. _____

B. _____

Note to the teacher: Use with the *Owl Moon* unit that begins on page 152.

Pigs in the Mud in the Middle of the Rud

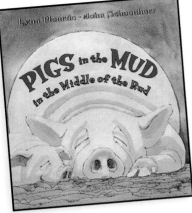

Written by Lynn Plourde
Illustrated by John Schoenherr

In this rollicking tale, a family outing in a Model T Ford is interrupted by a number of critters in the muddy roadway. Each family member, in turn, tries to shoo the animals, but it's all to no avail. That is, until Grandma gets her dander up and sends the critters scurrying.

Skill: Produce rhyming words.

Teacher Preparation

Literature selection: Preview a copy of *Pigs in the Mud in the Middle of the Rud.*

Craft:
- If desired, cover students' work area with newspaper for easy cleanup. Set out shallow containers of brown tempera paint.
- Cut several kitchen sponges into small pieces. Clip a clothespin onto each piece. Set at least one prepared sponge by each container.
- Make a desired number of 4$\frac{1}{2}$-inch and eight-inch circle templates for students to share.
- Gather the remaining student materials listed below.
- For the literacy link on the following page, gather a class supply of blank cards. On each card, write a different word for which there is at least one common rhyming word.

Extension: If desired, make a copy of page 159 for each student to complete at the conclusion of the unit.

Student Materials

Each student needs the following:
- copy of page 158
- access to a 4$\frac{1}{2}$" and an 8" circle template
- 9" x 12" sheet of pink construction paper
- 6" x 9" piece of pink construction paper
- 6" length of pink pipe cleaner
- access to brown tempera paint and a prepared sponge (See instructions above.)
- wide black marker
- scissors
- glue
- tape

Begin With a Book

Pigs in the Mud in the Middle of the Rud

Aah! To a pig there's nothing quite like the cool comfort of mud! Have students brainstorm what they know about pigs, prompting them as needed to note that pigs like mud. Then show students the book cover and read the title aloud. Direct students' attention to the word *rud*. Invite them to guess what it means. As you read the book aloud, have students check their guesses. Then help them use the context to confirm the word's meaning *(road)*. Distribute the materials listed on page 156. Ask each youngster to refer to the illustrated steps as you use the directions below to help her make a mud-loving pig.

Continue With a Craft

Muddy Pig Buddy

Directions:
1. Have each student use the black marker to trace a small and a large template on the provided pink paper.
2. Instruct her to cut along the outer edge of each tracing.
3. Ask her to glue the small circle onto the large circle to resemble a head.
4. Have her draw two eyes, a nose, and two ears with the marker as illustrated below.
5. Instruct her to wrap the pipe cleaner length around the marker to make a curly tail. Ask her to tape the tail to the back of the pig.
6. Invite her to sponge-paint the pig so that it looks muddy.

Link With a Literacy Skill

Pigs in the Rud

Students will go hog-wild over this rhyme-filled activity! Divide the class in half. Have the students in each half sit side by side to form a line facing the other half. (If you have an odd number of students, have two students in one line face one student in the other.) Ask each student in one line to hold her completed pig. Give each student in the other line a programmed card. To begin, have the first cardholder announce her word and show it to the facing student. Ask this student to name a rhyming word. Then lead the class in the chant shown, inserting the name of the next cardholder in line. Continue the process until the last pair (trio) of students has announced its rhymes. Lead the class in saying the chant, inserting "Grandma" for the name. Then instruct the students in each half to trade roles and use the remaining word cards for another round of rhyming fun.

Oh, no. Won't do. Gotta shoo. But who? [Student's name] will shoo. That's who.

157

Muddy Pig Buddy

Follow the directions.

1. Trace.

2. Cut along the outside of the lines.

3. Glue.

4. Draw two eyes, a nose, and two ears.

5. Wrap to make a tail.

6. Turn the pig over. Tape the tail.

7. Use a sponge to paint.

Note to the teacher: Use with the *Pigs in the Mud in the Middle of the Rud* unit that begins on page 156.

Name _____

Time for Supper!

Help the family get to supper!
Start at the car.
Look at the word bank.
Write a word that rhymes in each box.

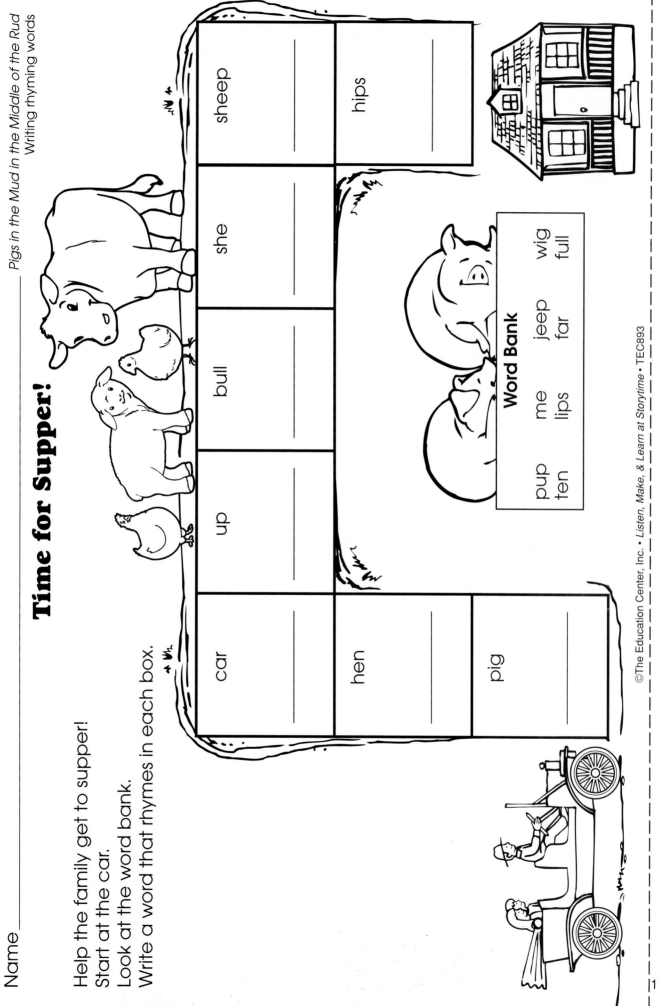

car	up	bull	she	sheep
___	___	___	___	___

hen				hips
___				___

pig
___

Word Bank

pup	me	jeep	wig
ten	lips	far	full

©The Education Center, Inc. • *Listen, Make, & Learn at Storytime* • TEC893

Note to the teacher: Use with the *Pigs in the Mud in the Middle of the Rud* unit that begins on page 156.

Quick As a Cricket

Quick as a Cricket
by Audrey Wood · illustrated by Don Wood
Child's Play

Written by Audrey Wood
Illustrated by Don Wood

A young boy creates a vivid description of himself when he turns to the animal kingdom for fitting comparisons. Brief rhyming text composed of clearly illustrated similes makes this predictable book a favorite among young children.

Skill: Use descriptive words and phrases.

Teacher Preparation

Literature selection: Preview a copy of *Quick As a Cricket*.

Craft:

- Obtain enough self-hardening modeling clay or dough to provide each student with a ball that is about the size of a child's fist. (If desired, prepare homemade dough. To do so, combine two cups of flour, one cup of salt, and enough water to make an easy-to-handle dough for every seven or eight students.)

- Make one or two copies of page 163 to make a class supply of cards. Cut apart the cards.

- After students' models are dry, set out shallow containers of tempera paint in various colors. Place at least one paintbrush beside each container.

- Gather the remaining student materials listed below.

Student Materials

Each student needs the following:
- copy of page 162
- animal card from page 163
- small portion of self-hardening modeling clay or dough
- piece of waxed paper, approximately 12" square
- access to tempera paint and paintbrushes
- access to assorted arts-and-crafts supplies, such as wiggle eyes, pom-poms, and yarn
- glue
- scissors

Begin With a Book

Quick As a Cricket

The descriptions in this charming book evoke images that are as clear as day! Prompt a class discussion about the expression "quiet as a mouse," inviting volunteers to tell about contexts in which they have heard it used. Explain that the featured book is about a boy who describes himself with animal-themed comparisons similar to this one. Read the book aloud. Then return to selected illustrations and confirm that students can distinguish between what the boy is imagining and what is actually happening. Next, give each student the materials listed on page 160. Check to be sure that each youngster is familiar with the animal pictured on his card. Have him refer to the illustrated steps as you use the directions below to guide him in making a model of his critter.

Continue With a Craft

Marvelous Animal Model

Directions:

1. Have each youngster use his waxed paper as a workmat. Ask him to silently read his card and study the illustration.
2. Instruct him to make a clay or dough model of his assigned animal and then have him set it aside until it is completely dry. (It might be necessary to reposition some models after several hours to allow all surfaces to dry.)
3. Instruct the youngster to paint the model. Let the paint dry.
4. Direct the student to use the provided arts-and-crafts materials to add desired details.

Link With a Literacy Skill

Delightful Descriptions

The menagerie in *Quick As a Cricket* inspires powerful descriptive phrases. No doubt your students' critters will spark vivid descriptions too! Gather students with their models in a circle on the floor. Reread the book. Then point out that the boy focuses on just one trait of each animal, such as the quickness of a cricket. For each of several featured animals, invite students to brainstorm words that describe traits the boy did not mention.

Next, have each student, in turn, show his classmates his model and describe the animal with two or three words. Give each youngster a 5" x 8" index card and have him return to his seat. Ask him to fold the card in half lengthwise and then write a sentence to describe his assigned animal. Display each youngster's model with the corresponding sentence on a low shelf or table. If desired, ask older students to describe themselves with similes inspired by the collection of critters.

A cat is cuddly, playful, and lazy.

Marvelous Animal Model

Follow the directions.

1. Place the waxed paper. Look at your card.

2. Roll.

3. Shape to make the animal. Let the animal dry.

4. Paint. Let the paint dry.

5. Glue to finish the animal.

©The Education Center, Inc. • *Listen, Make, & Learn at Storytime* • TEC893

Note to the teacher: Use with the *Quick As a Cricket* unit that begins on page 160.

Patterns

Use with the *Quick As a Cricket* unit that begins on page 160.

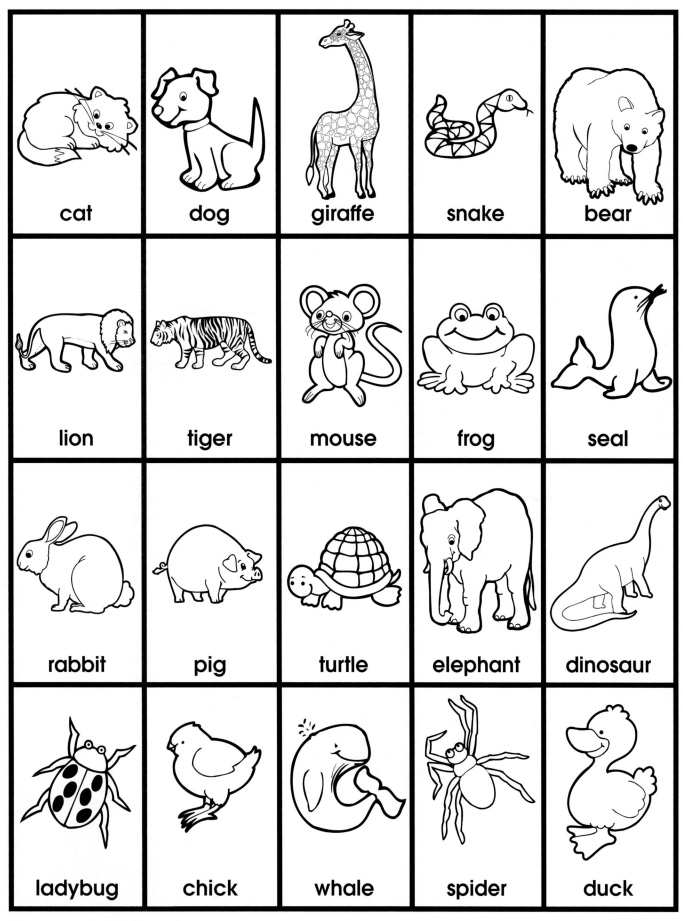

cat	dog	giraffe	snake	bear
lion	tiger	mouse	frog	seal
rabbit	pig	turtle	elephant	dinosaur
ladybug	chick	whale	spider	duck

Rechenka's Eggs

Written and illustrated by Patricia Polacco

Babushka works long and hard throughout the cold winter to paint exquisitely detailed eggs for the Easter Festival. One day an injured goose that she is nursing back to health accidentally breaks the eggs. What appears at first to be a great disappointment for the old woman leads to a miracle when the goose repays Babushka's kindness with the most beautiful eggs ever.

Skills: Listen for details. Make connections.

Teacher Preparation

Literature selection: Preview a copy of *Rechenka's Eggs*. Use a sticky note to mark the two-page spread that shows Babushka blowing out the eggs that Rechenka laid.

Craft:

- Set out watercolor pencils, thin paintbrushes, and small containers of water for students to share. If desired, place a supply of paper towels nearby.

- Gather the remaining student materials below.

- Make one copy of page 167 for the literacy link on the following page. Draw several writing lines in the blank space. Make three copies of the prepared sheet for each student.

Student Materials

Each student needs the following:
- copy of page 166
- white tagboard copy of page 167 (unlined)
- access to watercolor pencils, a thin paintbrush, and water
- nonwashable crayons
- scissors
- pencil

Begin With a Book

Rechenka's Eggs

When Babushka discovers Rechenka's first brilliantly colored egg, she declares it a miracle. Tell students that a *miracle* is an amazing event that cannot be explained. Reveal that a miracle occurs in the story that you are about to read. Display the book cover and read the title. Invite youngsters to predict what miracle will happen. Ask them to check their predictions as you share the book. Then have them compare the predictions with the story details.

Next, revisit the pages marked with the sticky note and ask youngsters to look closely at the designs on the eggs. Explain that each student will illustrate an egg with similar designs. Give each youngster the materials listed on page 164. Have her follow the illustrated steps as you use the directions below to guide her in the project.

Continue With a Craft

"Egg-cellent" Designs

1. Have each student use a pencil to lightly draw a desired design in the blank space of the tagboard egg.
2. Instruct her to firmly trace all the lines with nonwashable crayons.
3. Direct her to color the design with watercolor pencils.
4. Ask her to use a wet paintbrush to brush water lightly over the colored areas. (Caution her to rinse the paintbrush before brushing over a different color.) Allow the project to dry.
5. Have the youngster cut out the egg.

Link With a Literacy Skill

Extraordinary!

Who would have guessed that an old woman and a goose would become dear friends? Enhance students' understanding of the characters' extraordinary relationship with this picturesque writing project. Tell students that the book reveals a lot about Babushka and Rechenka through both pictures and words. During a second reading, ask students to listen and look closely to learn about the characters and the qualities that make them good friends. Then give each youngster three copies of the lined egg pattern.

The student cuts out the eggs. She titles one egg "Babushka" and one egg "Rechenka." She describes each character on the corresponding egg, supporting any inferences with story details. She labels the third egg with the name of someone who reminds her of one of the characters. Then she writes to explain what the person and the character have in common. If desired, the youngster may use crayons to color the designs on the eggs. To complete her project, she staples the resulting pages behind the decorated tagboard egg.

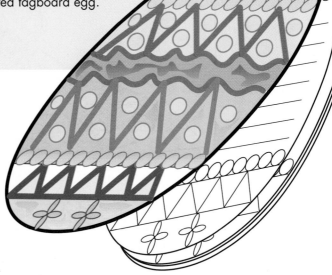

165

"Egg-cellent" Designs

Follow the directions.

① Draw.

② Use crayons to trace.

③ Use watercolor pencils to color.

④ Dip. Brush. Let dry.

⑤ Cut.

Note to the teacher: Use with the *Rechenka's Eggs* unit that begins on page 164.

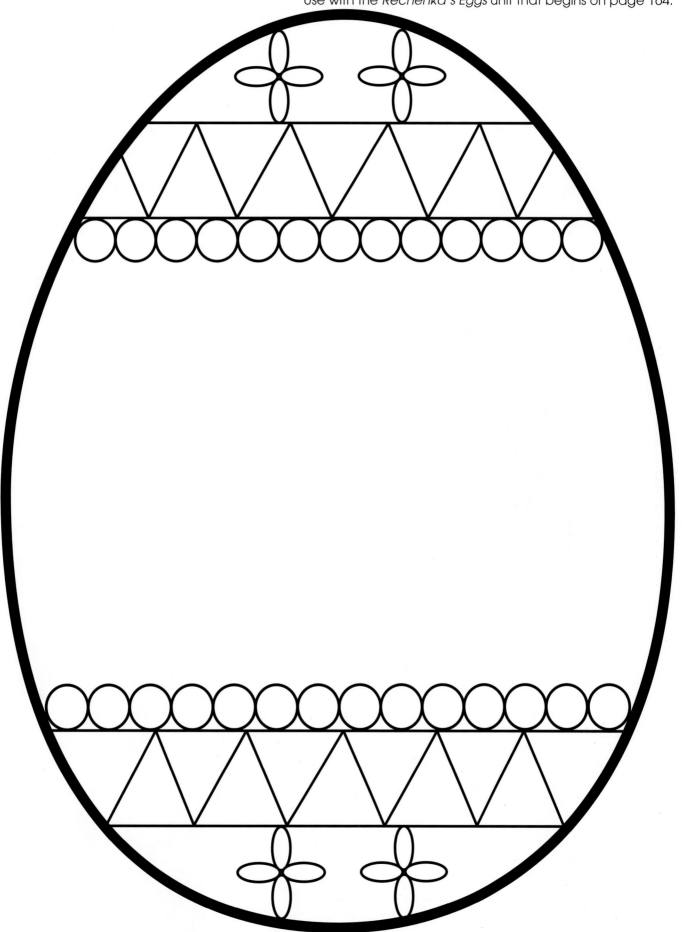

Sheep in a Jeep

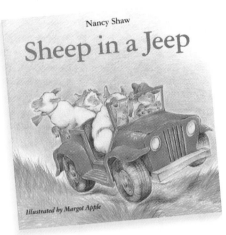

Written by Nancy Shaw
Illustrated by Margot Apple

Five sheep happily set out in a jeep for a ride in the country, never expecting the mishaps that lie in store for them. Simple rhyming text and humorous colored-pencil illustrations draw young listeners into the sheep's silly misadventures.

Skill: Read predictable text.

Teacher Preparation

Literature selection: Preview a copy of *Sheep in a Jeep*.

Craft:
- Gather the student materials listed below.

- For the literacy link activity on the following page, use large letters to program a separate blank card for each of these words: *bird, hill, frog, pigs,* and *mud*. Each student will need crayons for the activity.

Student Materials

Each student needs the following:
- copy of page 170
- tan or gray construction paper copy of the sheep pattern on page 171
- copy of the boxes on page 171
- five 6" x 9" pieces of white construction paper
- 6" x 9" piece of colored construction paper
- 2" length of yarn
- small jingle bell
- 3–4 white cotton balls
- access to a stapler
- scissors
- glue

Begin With a Book

Sheep in a Jeep

Take a wild and woolly ride with a flock of sheep! Display the book cover and read the title aloud. Prompt a class discussion about whether sheep can really drive, leading students to conclude that the book is a fantasy story. Then ask youngsters to imagine what problems sheep might encounter if they were able to drive. Invite them to share their thoughts. As you read the story aloud, encourage students to listen to find out what problems the author imagines. Then, to make a woolly reminder of the zany jeep ride, give each student the materials listed on page 168. Have him refer to the illustrated directions as you use the steps below to guide him in completing his project.

Step 1

Continue With a Craft

Woolly Sheep Booklet

Step 2

Directions:
1. Have each child cut out the patterns.
2. Tell him to glue the yarn length on the sheep's neck to resemble a collar. Direct him to glue the jingle bell on the lower end of the yarn.
3. Instruct him to stretch out the cotton balls and then glue them to the sheep's head and body as shown.
4. Ask him to position the colored construction paper horizontally to make a booklet cover. Have him glue on the sheep and the box that has the booklet title.
5. Ask him to stack the white paper, place the cover atop the stack, and staple the entire stack along the left-hand side.
6. Instruct him to glue the remaining boxes on the pages in numerical order, one box per page.

Step 3

Link With a Literacy Skill

Sheep Shenanigans

Set students on the road to reading fun with this activity inspired by *Sheep in a Jeep*! Remind students that signs are posted on roadways to help people drive safely. Suggest that the sheep's drive might have gone more smoothly if their roads had signs warning them of what was up ahead. To review the story sights, show students a prepared card. Have the students chorally read the word and then lead them in saying "See the [word on card]. Beep! Beep!" Repeat the process with the remaining word cards. To provide practice reading the featured words in context, pair students and have each youngster read his booklet to his partner. Encourage each youngster to illustrate his pages before he takes his booklet home to share with his family. Beep! Beep! What a reading treat!

One Sheep in a Jeep

Woolly Sheep Booklet

Follow the directions.

1. Cut.

2. Glue the yarn. Glue the bell.

3. Pull the cotton. Glue.

4. Glue the sheep. Glue the title.

5. Stack. Staple.

6. Glue in order.

Note to the teacher: Use with the *Sheep in a Jeep* unit that begins on page 168.

Patterns

Use with the *Sheep in a Jeep* unit that begins on page 168.

**One Sheep in
a Jeep**

©The Education Center, Inc.

See the bird.
Beep! Beep!

1.

See the hill.
Beep! Beep!

2.

See the frog.
Beep! Beep!

3.

See the pigs.
Beep! Beep!

4.

See the mud.
Beep! Beep!
Uh-oh!

5.

Snow

Retold and illustrated by Uri Shulevitz

A boy's anticipation for snow grows even though adults dismiss his belief that wintry weather is on its way. Caldecott Honor–winning illustrations and simple text capture the gradual transformation of the bleak cityscape into a snow-white winter wonderland.

Skill: Create an illustration and write an appropriate caption.

Teacher Preparation

Literature selection: Preview a copy of *Snow*.

Craft:
- In a shallow container, combine powdered Ivory Snow detergent with enough water to make a mixture that is the consistency of paint. (Allow one tablespoon of detergent per child.)

- Cover students' work area with newspaper for easy cleanup, if desired.

- Gather the remaining student materials listed below.

- For the literacy link on the following page, each student will need a 12" x 18" sheet of black construction paper and a sentence strip.

Student Materials

Each student needs the following:
- copy of pages 174 and 175
- 9" x 12" sheet of gray construction paper
- Ivory Snow detergent mixture (See instructions above.)
- access to construction paper scraps
- cotton swab
- pencil
- crayons
- scissors
- glue

Begin With a Book

Snow

Step 1

Share the joy and wonder of snow with this wintry story of anticipation! Tell students that Uri Shulevitz is both the author and illustrator of *Snow*. Confirm that they understand the roles of authors and illustrators in creating picture books. As you read the book aloud, ask students to think about how the words and pictures work together to tell the story. Then invite volunteers to share their observations.

Next, revisit each page with students to examine the artwork more closely. Point out that the drab colors throughout most of the book create a striking contrast with the white and blue snow-covered scenes at the conclusion. Then give each student the materials listed on page 172. Have her refer to the illustrated directions as you use the steps below to guide her in making her own wintry scene.

Continue With a Craft

Snowy Scene

Step 2

Directions:

1. Have each student color the cityscape pattern as desired and then cut it out.
2. Direct her to glue it onto the sheet of gray construction paper.
3. Ask her to use crayons to add details to the scene. To further embellish the picture, invite her to draw and color people, animals, or objects on the construction paper scraps. Then have her cut them out and glue them on her paper.
4. Instruct her to dip the cotton swab into the detergent mixture and then dab dots on her picture to make snowflakes. Have her repeat the process until she is satisfied with the result. Allow the artwork to dry.

Link With a Literacy Skill

Wintertime Captions

Step 3

The forecast is for a flurry of writing and reading fun! Remind students that a good author-illustrator uses words and pictures that complement each other. To illustrate this point, revisit selected pages from *Snow*. Then give each youngster a 12" x 18" sheet of black construction paper and a sentence strip. Have her position the construction paper horizontally on a work surface and glue her completed scene in the center of it. Ask her to write on the sentence strip a caption that is appropriate for her artwork. (Or have her dictate a caption and write it for her.) Show the class each student's artwork, in turn, as she reads her caption aloud. Display each illustration above its caption on a hall wall; then title the resulting winter wonderland "Sensational Snowy Scenes."

It was snowing hard in the city.

Snowy Scene

Follow the directions.

1

Color.

2

Cut out.

3

Glue.

4

Add details.

5

Dip. Dab to make snowflakes.

6

Dip again. Make more snowflakes. Let the picture dry.

Note to the teacher: Use with the *Snow* unit that begins on page 172.

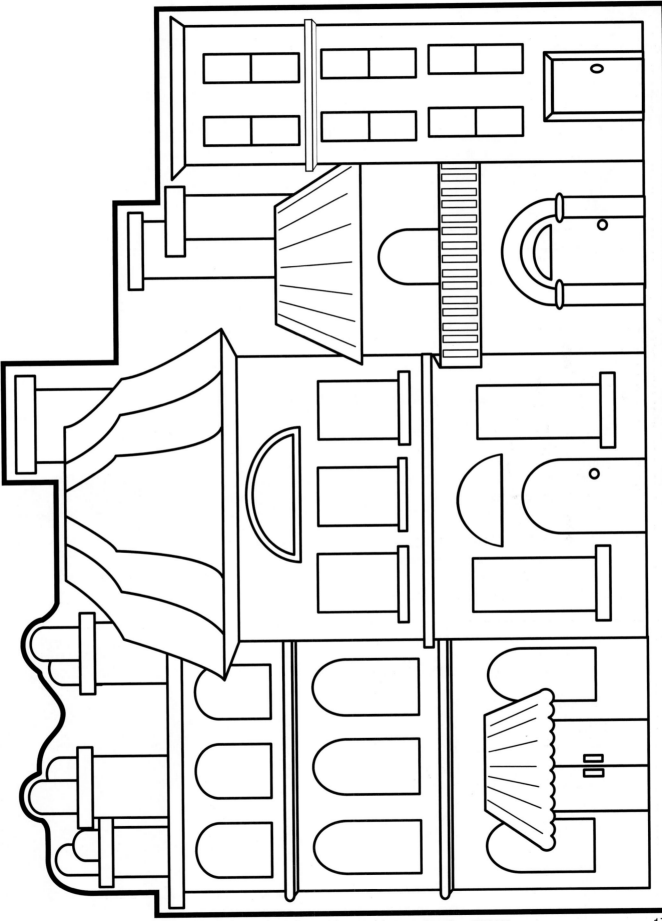

Strega Nona

Retold and illustrated by Tomie dePaola

Big Anthony discovers the secret of Strega Nona's magic pasta pot. Or so he thinks! When he tries to impress the townsfolk by using the magic pot, it quickly becomes apparent that there is more to Strega Nona's secret than he thinks. Award-winning illustrations humorously depict the nearly disastrous results of Big Anthony's attempt at magic and the satisfying resolution.

Skill: Identify and read words that start with p.

Teacher Preparation

Literature selection: Preview a copy of *Strega Nona*.

Craft:
- Obtain enough uncooked spaghetti to allow two full-length pieces per student. Break the pieces in half and then cook them according to the package directions. Rinse the cooked spaghetti with cold water.

- Cover students' work area with newspaper for easy cleanup, if desired. Set out several colors of tempera paint.

- Gather the remaining student materials listed below.

- Make a large gray cooking pot cutout for the literacy link on the following page and label it "Pasta Pot of P Words."

Student Materials

Each student needs the following:
- copy of page 178
- 1–4 pieces of cooked spaghetti
- 9" x 12" sheet of tagboard
- 1 copy of the programmed booklet page and 4 copies of the unprogrammed booklet page on page 179
- tempera paint
- 6" x 9" piece of brown construction paper
- 2" x 6" piece of gray construction paper
- pencil
- glue
- permanent marker
- scissors
- access to a stapler

Begin With a Book

Step 1

Strega Nona

What do you get when you combine one inattentive character and a magic pasta pot? A tempting tale with a valuable lesson about following directions! Show students the book cover. Direct their attention to the cooking pot and explain that it is a magic pasta pot. Confirm that students know what the word *pasta* means. Then tell them that a character named Big Anthony touches the pasta pot even though he is warned not to. Ask students to predict what happens. Read the book aloud. After comparing students' predictions with the story events, revisit selected illustrations of the bubbling pasta. Then give each student the materials listed on page 176. Have him refer to the illustrated directions as you use the steps below to guide him in "boiling" up a pasta-style booklet.

Continue With a Craft

Step 2

Pasta Painting

Directions:
1. Have each youngster dip a piece of spaghetti in the paint and then repeatedly pull it across the tagboard to make a design.
2. Have him continue dipping and painting as desired. Allow the paint to dry.
3. Instruct him to fold the tagboard in half to 6" x 9", unfold it, and then cut along the crease to make booklet covers.
4. Direct him to stack the reproducible programmed page atop the unprogrammed pages and then staple the entire stack between the covers.
5. Ask him to draw a fork on the gray paper, cut it out, and sign it.
6. Instruct him to cut several meatball shapes from the brown paper.
7. Have him glue the meatballs and fork on the front cover.

Link With a Literacy Skill

Step 3

A Pasta Pot of *P* Words

Cook up reading practice with Strega Nona's magic pot! After each student has made a booklet as described above, ask him to turn to the first page. Read the poem as a class; then display the prepared pot cutout. As students brainstorm words that begin with *p*, record the words on the cutout. Next, ask each youngster to copy a different brainstormed word on each page of his booklet. Have him practice reading the completed booklet to a classmate. Then encourage students to take their booklets home for more mouthwatering reading fun.

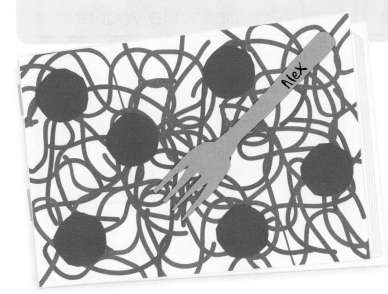

Pasta Pot of <u>P</u> Words

pig	pony
play	pool
please	paint
pet	princess

Pasta Painting

Follow the directions.

1 Dip.

2 Paint with the pasta.

3 Dip again. Paint more. Let the paint dry.

4 Fold. Unfold the paper; then cut it in half.

5 Stack the pages. Staple.

6 Cut a fork from the gray paper. Write your name.

7 Cut meatballs from the brown paper.

8 Glue.

©The Education Center, Inc. • *Listen, Make, & Learn at Storytime* • TEC893

178   **Note to the teacher:** Use with the *Strega Nona* unit that begins on page 176.

Bubble, bubble, pasta pot.
Boil up some *p* words, nice and hot.
I'm ready and it's time to look
At all the words in my pasta book!

Tops & Bottoms

Adapted and illustrated by Janet Stevens

Bear discovers it's a mistake to go into business with a neighbor, especially when the neighbor is as tricky as Hare! While Bear lazes on his porch, Hare cleverly fools him into taking the least useful parts of three different crops. Caldecott Honor–winning illustrations on vertical two-page spreads portray the neighbors with humor and charm.

Skill: Categorize words.

Teacher Preparation

Literature selection: Preview a copy of *Tops & Bottoms*.

Craft:
- Collect a class supply of clean, empty half-pint milk containers. Use a craft knife to cut off the top portion of each container, leaving approximately two inches.

- Cover students' work area with newspaper for easy cleanup.

- Set out shallow containers of brown tempera paint.

- Gather the remaining student materials listed below.

- For the literacy link on the following page, make a copy of page 183 for each student.

Student Materials

Each student needs the following:
- copy of page 182
- prepared half-pint milk container (See instructions above.)
- 1¹/₂" black construction paper circle
- brown tempera paint
- 2 Popsicle sticks
- paintbrush
- masking tape

Begin With a Book

Tops & Bottoms

When it comes to trickster tales, this book is the pick of the crop! Read the title aloud, then preview the story with students by looking at the pictures and discussing them. Ask students to share their ideas about why the author chose the title *Tops & Bottoms*. Then read the book aloud. Guide students as necessary to understand that the title refers to parts of vegetables. Have students recall the vegetables that Hare grew and how he categorized them by the parts that most appealed to him. To further explore ways to categorize vegetables, give each student the materials listed on page 180. Ask the youngster to refer to the illustrated steps as you use the provided directions to help her make a mini wheelbarrow for the literacy link below.

Continue With a Craft

Handy Wheelbarrow

Directions:

1. Instruct each child to place the prepared carton on its side. Have her place a Popsicle stick horizontally on the top panel so that one end is flush with one edge of the carton. Ask her to tape the stick in place to make a handle. (See the illustration below.)
2. Direct her to flip the carton. Have her position and tape the second Popsicle stick to make another handle.
3. Ask her to paint the sides of the carton brown, including where the sticks are taped. Allow the paint to dry.
4. Use a craft knife to make a slit in the middle of the front panel's bottom edge.
5. Ask the student to carefully insert the construction paper circle into the slit to make a wheel.

Link With a Literacy Skill

Veggie Sort

There's no doubt about it—Hare has a clever way of categorizing vegetables! To find out how your students categorize them, give each student a copy of page 183. Confirm that students know the name and color of each pictured vegetable. Have them brainstorm categories for sorting the vegetables, such as colors and initial letters. Ask each youngster to color her vegetables, cut them out, and then place them in her wheelbarrow.

Next, pair students. Have one youngster in each twosome remove her vegetables from her wheelbarrow and sort them into categories of her choice. Challenge her partner to identify the categories. After she successfully identifies them, ask the students to trade roles. Now that's an activity sure to harvest bushels of critical thinking!

lettuce   green bean

Handy Wheelbarrow

Follow the directions.

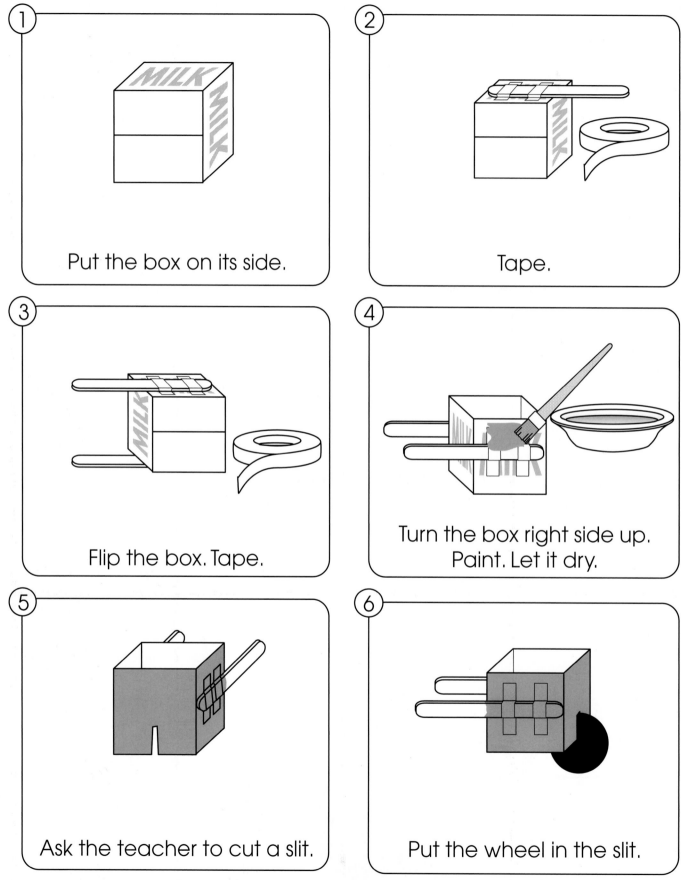

1. Put the box on its side.

2. Tape.

3. Flip the box. Tape.

4. Turn the box right side up. Paint. Let it dry.

5. Ask the teacher to cut a slit.

6. Put the wheel in the slit.

Note to the teacher: Use with the *Tops & Bottoms* unit that begins on page 180.

carrot	peas	radish	cauliflower
broccoli	potato	lettuce	green bean
corn	tomato	beet	celery

The Very Hungry Caterpillar

Written and illustrated by Eric Carle

Each day for a week, a seemingly insatiable caterpillar eats increasingly larger amounts of food. He then retreats into a cocoon to rest (and to recover from a very full belly!). A couple of weeks later, he emerges from the cocoon as a bright and colorful butterfly. Vibrant collage illustrations and simple text on die-cut pages tell this remarkable story of metamorphosis.

Skill: Read simple, high-frequency words.

Teacher Preparation

Literature selection: Preview a copy of *The Very Hungry Caterpillar*.

Craft:

- Gather a class supply of empty toilet tissue tubes. Use a hole puncher to make two holes in each tube as illustrated.

- Make several wing templates like the one shown.

- Set out assorted colors of tempera paint in shallow containers. Place an eyedropper beside each color.

- Cover students' work area with newspaper.

- Gather the remaining student materials listed below.

- For the literacy link activity on the following page, prepare a number of construction paper leaf cut-outs. Program each one with a different day of the week, color word, or number word.

Extension: If desired, make a copy of page 187 for each student to complete at the conclusion of the unit.

Student Materials

Each student needs the following:

- copy of page 186
- prepared cardboard tube (See instructions above.)
- 9" x 12" sheet of white construction paper
- access to a wing template
- clothespin
- assorted colors of tempera paint, each with an eyedropper
- paintbrush
- pipe cleaner
- scissors
- pencil

Begin With a Book
The Very Hungry Caterpillar

From a tiny egg to a breathtaking butterfly, a caterpillar's life cycle unfolds in this beloved classic! Tell students that you will read a book about a caterpillar that is very hungry. Invite them to share their ideas about what the caterpillar might eat. Read the story aloud to check their predictions. Next, point out that most real caterpillars eat green plants, not foods such as those in the book. Explain that caterpillars eat a lot because they need energy to become butterflies. Tell students that this change is called *metamorphosis*. Then give each youngster the materials listed on page 184. Have him refer to the illustrated directions as you help him make a very hungry caterpillar of his own.

Step 1

Continue With a Craft
Crafty Caterpillar

Step 2

Directions:
1. Have each child clip a clothespin to his tube to serve as a handle.
2. Instruct him to paint the tube. Then have him remove the clothespin and set the tube aside to dry.
3. Direct him to fold his paper in half. Then have him align the wing template on the fold and trace the wing. Ask him to cut out the tracing and then unfold it.
4. Have him use the eyedroppers to place several drops of paint on one wing. Instruct him to fold the wings in half and press them together. Tell him to unfold the wings and set them aside.
5. Instruct him to thread his pipe cleaner through the holes in his painted tube. Ask him to twist the pipe cleaner to secure it in place and then shape it to resemble antennae.

Link With a Literacy Skill
"Crunch-a, Munch-a!"

Step 3

Your students' caterpillars don't like to eat yummy treats like the caterpillar in the story does. They like to munch on words instead! Gather students in a circle on the floor. Have each student wear his completed caterpillar on two fingers like a puppet. Place the leaf cutouts faceup in the center of the circle. Invite a volunteer to pick up a selected leaf with his free hand and pretend to have his caterpillar read it aloud. Then have him return the leaf. Continue around the circle in this manner until every student has taken one turn. Announce that after this meal of leafy words, the caterpillars are ready to turn into butterflies! Then arrange for each student to glue his wings to his caterpillar to transform it into a fancy flier. Amazing!

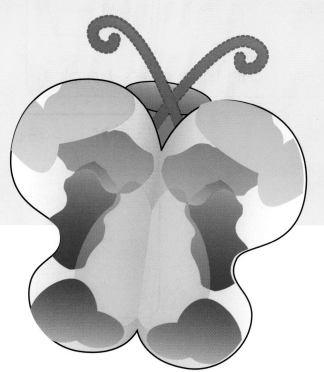

Crafty Caterpillar

Follow the directions.

1 Clip.

2 Paint. Let dry.

3 Fold. Trace. Cut.

4 Unfold. Place drops of paint.

5 Fold and then press. Unfold.

6 Poke the pipe cleaner through the holes. Twist.

7 **Later** Glue on the wings.

Note to the teacher: Use with *The Very Hungry Caterpillar* unit that begins on page 184.

Munch, Munch, Munch!

Color.
Cut out the boxes.
Glue each box on the correct leaf.

Days

Number Words

©The Education Center, Inc. • *Listen, Make, & Learn at Storytime* • TEC893

Sunday	one	Friday	Wednesday
six	Monday	eight	ten

Note to the teacher: Use with *The Very Hungry Caterpillar* unit that begins on page 184.

Zin! Zin! Zin! a Violin

Written by Lloyd Moss
Illustrated by Marjorie Priceman

One by one, the members of an orchestra take their places on center stage. Gliding, soaring, swinging notes fill the air with each tuneful addition and culminate in a crowd-pleasing concert. Playful rhyming text presents a variety of music-related words and bounces across the pages along with lively, award-winning illustrations.

Skill: Categorize words.

Teacher Preparation

Literature selection: Preview a copy of *Zin! Zin! Zin! a Violin.*

Craft:

- Collect a class supply of clean, rectangular Styrofoam trays (or purchase inexpensive rectangular Styrofoam trays from a local paper- or party-supply store).

- For each student, use a craft knife to cut slits approximately one inch apart in the short ends of a Styrofoam tray.

- Gather the remaining student materials listed below.

- For the literacy link on the following page, list each of the following groups of words on a separate sheet of small chart paper: *one, three, six, nine; horn, violin, trumpet, flute;* and *sings, stings, strings.*

Extension: If desired, make a copy of page 191 for each student to complete at the conclusion of the literacy link activity described on page 189.

Student Materials

Each student needs the following:
- copy of page 190
- prepared rectangular Styrofoam tray (See instructions above.)
- 3" x 12" poster board or tagboard strip
- crayons or markers
- masking tape
- string
- scissors

Begin With a Book

Zin! Zin! Zin! a Violin

Strengthen students' vocabularies with this tuneful story! To preview the book, show students each page, prompting discussion about the instruments and introducing the names of any that are unfamiliar to them. Read the book aloud. Then reread the book, pausing at the name of each instrument and inviting students to chime in. Next, tell students that each of them will make a zany stringed instrument. Give each student the materials listed on page 188. Have her follow the illustrated steps as you use the directions below to guide her in completing the project.

Step 1

Continue With a Craft

Zany Stringed Instrument

1. Instruct each child to tape one end of the string to the back of the Styrofoam tray.
2. Direct her to thread the string through the first slit, bring it across the front of the plate, and pull it down through the opposite slit. Have her continue winding the string around the Styrofoam tray in this manner until it has been threaded through every slit.
3. Ask her to cut the string and tape it to the back.
4. To make a fingerboard, have her use markers or crayons to color the provided strip as desired.
5. Have her tape the fingerboard to the back so that the colored side faces the front of the tray.

Step 2

Link With a Literacy Skill

In Perfect Harmony

Step 3

This book's harmonious blend of number, music, and rhyming words is right in tune with categorization practice! Display the previously prepared sheets of chart paper and tell students that the words are from the story. Lead the class in reading aloud the lists and confirm that students understand the meanings of the words. Next, ask each student to stand and hold her homemade stringed instrument. Instruct her to gently strum it as you lead the class in singing the song below. Then have students chorally read a chosen list of words. Invite volunteers to share their ideas about the category to which the listed words belong. After the correct category is identified, repeat the singing and reading process with the two remaining lists. Now that's a "note-able" way to boost vocabulary skills!

Word Wonder
(sung to the tune of "Twinkle, Twinkle, Little Star")

A, B, C, and 1, 2, 3,
Let's read the words that we see.
Make a guess—tell what's the same.
That's the secret to this game.
A, B, C, and 1, 2, 3,
Let's read the words that we see.

Zany Stringed Instrument

Follow the directions.

① Tape to the back of the tray.

② Wind the string around.

③ Pass the string from slit to slit.

④ Cut. Tape.

⑤ Color.

⑥ Tape to the back.

⑦ Play!

Note to the teacher: Use with the *Zin! Zin! Zin! a Violin* unit that begins on page 188.

Name _____

Name _____

Zin! Zin! Zin! a Violin
Categorizing words

Word Trios

Read. Label each list with one word.
Draw an **X** on the list that shows things for playtime.

apple
orange
banana

dog
cat
fish

ball
block
doll

Bonus Box: On the back of this sheet, write two more words for each list. Draw and color a picture for each word.

©The Education Center, Inc. • *Listen, Make, & Learn at Storytime* • TEC893

Note to the teacher: Use with the *Zin! Zin! Zin! a Violin* unit that begins on page 188.

191

Storytime News

_____
date

Today we read

_____
title

_____

by

_____
author

Then I made a project to go with the story!

Look At What I Made!

This craft will help me remember that we read

_____
title

_____

by

_____.
author

Ask me to tell you about it!

Today's Storytime

_____
date

We read _____

_____

by _____.

Then we made a craft.
Ask me to show it to you,
and I'll tell you about the story!

192

Note to the teacher: Upon completion of a unit in this book, make a copy of this page. Complete a selected form with the appropriate information. Then send a copy of the program form home with each student.